SO-BFB-026

PASSPORT
THAILAND

Passport To The World

Passport Argentina
Passport Brazil
Passport China
Passport France
Passport Germany
Passport Hong Kong
Passport India
Passport Indonesia
Passport Israel
Passport Italy
Passport Japan
Passport Korea
Passport Mexico
Passport Philippines
Passport Russia
Passport Singapore
Passport South Africa
Passport Spain
Passport Taiwan
Passport United Kingdom
Passport USA
Passport Vietnam

PASSPORT THAILAND

Your Pocket Guide to Thai Business, Customs & Etiquette

Naomi Wise

Contributing Editor: L. Leland Whitney

Passport Series Editor: Barbara Szerlip

WORLD TRADE PRESS®
Professional Books for International Trade

World Trade Press
1505 Fifth Avenue
San Rafael, California 94901 USA
Tel: (415) 454-9934
Fax: (415) 453-7980
E-mail: WorldPress@aol.com
USA Order Line: (800) 833-8586

"Passport to the World" concept: Edward G. Hinkelman
Cover design: Peter Jones, Marge Wilhite
Illustrations: Tom Watson

Passport Thailand
Copyright © 1997 by World Trade Press. All Rights Reserved.

Reproduction of any part of this work beyond that permitted by
the United States Copyright Act without the express written permission of the copyright holder is unlawful. Requests for permission or further information should be addressed to World Trade
Press at the address above.

This publication is designed to provide general information concerning the cultural aspects of doing business with people from a
particular country. It is sold with the understanding that the pub-
lisher is not engaged in rendering legal or any other professional
services. If legal advice or other expert assistance is required, the
services of a competent professional person should be sought.

Library of Congress Cataloging-in-Publication Data
Wise, Naomi
Passport Thailand: your pocket guide to Thai business, customs
& etiquette / Naomi Wise
p. cm. -- ("Passport to the world")
Includes bibliographical references (p.)
ISBN 1-885073-26-7
1. Corporate culture -- Thailand. 2. Business etiquette -- Thailand.
3. Industrial management -- Social aspects -- Thailand. 4. Negotiation in business -- Thailand. 5. Intercultural communication. I.
Title. II. Series.
HD58.7.W57 1996
390'.009593--dc20
96-14869 CIP

Printed in the United States of America

Table of Contents
Thailand

Asia's Fifth Dragon

Thailand
Quick Look

Official name	Muang Thai or Prathet Thai
Land area	513,115 sq km (198,115 sq mi)
Capital & largest city	Bangkok (11+ million)
Elevations	Highest – 2,596 m (8,500 ft)
	Lowest–sea level

People
  Population (1995)   59.5 million
  Density   115 per sq km
  Distribution   20% urban, 80% rural
  Annual growth   1.4%
Official language   Thai
Major religions   Theravada Buddhism
Economy (1994 est.)
  GDP   US$323 billion
                             US$2500 per capita
  Foreign trade   Imports — US$40.8 billion
                             Exports — US$37.7 billion
  Principal trade partners   Japan
                             U.S.
                             Singapore
                             Germany
                             Taiwan
  Currency   1 baht = 100 santangs
  Exchange Rate (11/96)   25 baht = US$1
Education and health
  Literacy (1995)   93%
  Universities   17
  Life expectancy (1994)   Women – 71.9 years
                             Men –64.9 years
  Infant mortality (1994)   37.1 per 1,000 live births

THAILAND

1 Country Facts

Geography and Demographics

Resembling a nodding profile of the head of its royal animal, the elephant, Thailand extends some 1800 km (1000 mi), its trunk a long narrow peninsula that rides the Pacific between the Gulf of Thailand and the island-speckled Andaman Sea. It borders Cambodia and Vietnam on the east, Laos in the North, Myanmar (Burma) to the northwest, and Malaysia to the south. Thailand's 513,115-sq-km area (slightly under 200,000 sq mi) is about the same size as France or the state of Texas.

Archeological remains reveal that ancient Siam developed a Bronze Age civilization even earlier than Sumeria did. However, modern Thai arrived from Yunnan (in south China) during the 13th century, pushed south by Kubla Khan's Mongols. Historians suspect they may have migrated from Thailand to China in earlier times, and returned centuries later.

Although Bangkok's population has doubled in the last twenty years, making it one of the world's largest and most congested cities, 80 percent of the country's inhabitants remain in rural areas, mainly engaged in rice cultivation.

The population is approximately 84 percent Thai. Identifiable Chinese, about 12 percent, are the largest minority. A vast number of Thai have some Chinese ancestry; Sino-Thai families own most of the country's largest companies and nearly all the banks. But there's little ethnic discord because intermarriage is routine. (For more on the Sino-Thai, see pages 15 and 84). The remainder of the population includes some Malay, a scattering of East Indians, Khmers and Laotians, and semi-nomadic hill tribes with approximately half a million members.

The vast majority of Thai practice Theravada Buddhism; about 3 percent are Moslems, a relative few are Hindu or Sikh, and due to the attentions of missionaries, some hill tribes are nominally Christian. Forty-five percent of the country's population is under the age of sixteen.

Climate

Thailand, at the same latitude as Nicaragua, has three seasons: hot and humid, hot and drenching, and very warm. In summer (from March to May), there's high humidity but little rainfall, with average daytime temperatures hovering around 93°F (34°C). Extended heat spells reach as high as 105°F (40°C). Monsoon season (characterized by several brief but intense daily drenchings) begins in late May with a downpour and climaxes in September with rainfalls in Bangkok of up to 12 inches per day. Temperatures range from 80° to 89°F (2° to 32°C). The northeast receives the least rain, but the southern peninsula is flooded during monsoon. The "cool" dry winter is November through February, when the weather resembles the Caribbean or Hawaii, with light breezes, lower humidity, and daytime temperatures in the low to mid 80°s F (low

30°s C). In the hills of the north, nighttime temperatures can drop to 44°F (7°C). The best months for business visits are January and February. Little serious business gets transacted during the protracted December holiday season.

Business Hours

Business hours are 9 A.M. to 6 P.M., Monday through Friday, with lunch at noon. Some businesses open until noon on Saturday. Banks are open 9 A.M. to 3 P.M. weekdays, and large stores from 10 A.M. to 7 P.M. seven days a week.

National Holidays

New Year's Day . . . . January 1

People bring food to temple monks and sprinkle statues of Buddha with water. Before the Western-style New Year was adopted, these customs applied to Chinese New Year, which is now a day for family feasting and various entertainments.

Makha Bucha . . . . February/March*

Commemorates day Buddha first preached the way to enlightenment to his five original disciples. A day for such merit-making activities as buying and releasing caged birds, burning incense and candlelit processions. Beginning of a pilgrimage season.

Chakri Memorial Day . . . . . April 6

Celebrates founding of Chakri Dynasty, which currently reigns.

SonkranThai. . . . . New Year, three days in April*

A Buddhist religious festival that has evolved into a national water-throwing event.

National Labor Day . . . . May 1

Adopted from the West.

Coronation Day. . . . . May 5
> Honors the coronation of H.M. King Bhumibol in 1950.

Plowing Ceremony Day . . . . . . May/June*
> Hindu-based festival; in which the Lord of Plowing (one
> chosen in each village, priests do the honors in
> Bangkok) breaks the soil, scatters rice and begs for rain.
> Marks the beginning of rainy season.

Visakha Puja. . . . . May 13*
> Most sacred day of Buddhist calendar, honors Buddha's
> birth, enlightenment and death.

Asaha Puja or Khao Phansa . . July*
> Similar to Western Lent. Marks start of three-month
> Buddhist retreat season, during which many young
> men temporarily enter the priesthood.

Buddhist Lent Day . . . . July/August*

H.M. The Queen's Birthday. . . . August 12
> Also Mother's Day.

Kathin . . . . October/
                                       November*
> End of Buddhist Lent. The King rides on royal barge to
> deliver splendid robes to monks of the royal temples;
> monks are given new robes nationwide.

Festival of Chulalongkorn. . . . . October 23
> Honors the monarch who abolished slavery.

H.M. The King's Birthday . . . . . December 5
> Offices close for three days.

Constitution Day . . . . December 10
> Commemorates Thailand's Constitution, adopted in
> 1932.

New Year's Eve. . . . . December 31
> People clean their houses and burn the old year's trash.

*date varies, determined by lunar calendar

Additional regional holidays include Chiang
Mai Flower Festival and Surin's elephant round-
up. For more on holidays, see Chapter 16: Customs.

2 The Thai

Language

Like Chinese and Vietnamese, Thai is a tonal language. A single syllable will have a completely different meaning when spoken in a rising, level or falling tone. The word *sua*, for example, can mean *mat*, *shirt* or *tiger*, while *chai* can stand for *fringe*, *man*, *victory*, or a multitude of verbs. Implication and mood also play major roles.

The written script is based on Sanskrit and Pali — ancient Indian languages. Thai is poetic, filled with metaphors and adages. The hundred or more ethnic dialects, plus four major regional dialects, are mutually understandable (albeit with some difficulty). Because the government promotes the central Thai dialect in schools, there's concern in some quarters that Thailand's diverse linguistic heritage is facing extinction.

As a result of the tourist industry and Vietnam-era American military bases, English is a rapidly-spreading commercial language. Those relatively few Thai who are schooled beyond the 6th grade usually learn English in public secondary schools and universities. Some Thai also speak a smattering of German and/or Japanese.

Buddhism In Daily Life

Thailand is nearly 95 percent Theravada Buddhist (also called Hinayana), the closest sect to Buddha's original teachings. With no gods to worship (Buddha was both agnostic and mortal), no saints to pray to, nor even any rites for observing such personal milestones as birth and death, Theravada may seem austere, but the Thai practice it casually and joyfully — and it's a key to their personalities.

Like its ancestor, Hinduism, Buddhism centers on the concept of reincarnation. Each being is doomed to endless rebirth, but without memory of previous lives. (The reincarnating soul is like the last flame of a burnt-down candle lighting a new candle.) *Karma* (earned fate) determines the conditions of each rebirth. Even with the best *karma*, though, life is viewed as a state of suffering. The aim is not to *transcend* reality and *transform* the soul, as in the West, but to *embrace* reality and *erase* the soul — by escaping the Wheel of Life, or at least winning a better position on it. Vanquishing the ego (typically, by meditation) is the key to obtaining release (*Nirvana*) from the Wheel. Good deeds of a religious sort can earn 'merit' toward a better reincarnation.

By the age of twenty-five, nearly every solvent young man joins a *sangha* (monastery) for several months, to earn karmic merit for himself and his mother (since women may become nuns but can't be ordained). Employers grant a paid leave on a once-per-lifetime basis for this. The Thai also donate money, food, and labor to the *wats* (temple complexes) to earn merit. (Thailand has nearly 30,000 *wats*, 400 in Bangkok alone.) The *wats*, in turn, serve their communities with schools, social and charity centers, and crematoria. In old age, many Thai of both sexes enter *sanghas* to conclude their lives in meditation.

Like the creators of Europe's Medieval church arts, the makers of Siam's masterpieces were mainly anonymous. The glory went to Buddha (and to the ruler who commissioned the devout works), while to the artist went karmic merit points. As in earlier eras, today's art patrons support classical/religious art (which gains them merit), over modern art (which doesn't).

Along with Buddhist rituals, Thais engage in Hindu ceremonies for birth, marriage and cremation, and Brahmin astrologers provide advice about propitious dates for starting new ventures. Hinduism also provides mythic material for much Thai painting, drama, dance and classical literature, including the *Ramakien*, a Thai version of India's epic *Ramayana*. (The latter, rendered in a highly stylized dance-drama form called *lakhon*, complete with gorgeous masks and elaborate costumes, takes seventy-two hours to perform in full.)

Christian evangelism — with its premise of superiority over other forms of worship — is deeply discomfiting, if not shocking, from a Buddhist viewpoint. Still, Thais frown on intolerance, and they don't stand for religious disrespect. Westerners who've been so rash as to clamber onto the heads of the great Buddha statues to take snapshots have been fined and expelled — for the triple violation of touching the Buddha, taking his photograph, and worst of all, placing themselves above his head.

Spirit Houses

Coexisting with Buddhism are even more ancient beliefs. Each Thai home has both a guardian spirit and a doorsill spirit.

Guardian spirits are believed to be there by natural right, whereas humans are only incidental occupants of the land. Dollhouse-sized 'spirit houses' are often placed on pillars on the front lawn for them and draped with colorful garlands of flowers. The spirit is often represented by a small statue of a young man holding a bag of money (symbolizing prosperity) and a sword (to ward off evil).

Before setting up a spirit house, a Brahmin priest must ascertain the best location — never in the shadow of a building, where human and spirit worlds might mingle. A ceremony (chants and incantations) is also required; the number nine (highly auspicious) is usually featured in the time it takes place. Jewelry and coins are buried beneath the pillar, and a feast of sweets, betel nuts, rice whiskey, cigarettes and possibly a pig's head are laid out — all to entice the spirit into taking up residence.

Thailand's most famous spirit house is Erewan Shrine, built in 1956 after several construction workers died while working on a nearby Bangkok hotel. The accidents stopped immediately. Believed to hold special powers, Erewan Shrine is continually besieged by people seeking winning lottery tickets, work promotions and success at love.

Doorsill spirits are unpredictable and potentially malevolent. Stepping on (not over) the doorsill can bring misfortune, and such carelessness will definitely offend any Thai witnesses.

Respect for the King

U.S.-educated King Bhumibol inherited the throne in 1946. The world's longest reigning monarch, he's outlasted 15 constitutions, 17 military coups and 21 prime ministers. A jazz saxophonist, he wrote Thailand's royal anthem, "Falling Rain."

He is beloved by his people; be aware that Thais will find any criticism of him deeply offensive. To date, Bhumibol has initiated some 2,000 projects, mainly to improve the lives of rural villagers. He has the right to accept or veto new laws but hasn't exercised that power in years. Still, the royal family's immense moral suasion ensures that whichever side it takes is likely to be victorious.

The Family

Thais regard their parents with deep respect and affection, but in public life, family status has little effect on individual status.

Many rural couples live with their parents, with grandmother baby-sitting while both spouses work in the fields. Some urban young adults live with friends or distant relatives while contributing to the support of rural parents. However, with continued urbanization, the tradition of extended families living together under one roof is changing. Urban businesses often allow rural-born employees several days off following the Plowing Ceremony to visit home and help their families in the fields.

Although families are nominally male-headed, Thai culture is possibly the most matriarchal in all of Asia. Familial respect is accorded by age and religious merit, as well as by gender.

The Village: Work Is Play

A Thai proverb holds that even city-dwellers are villagers at heart. Most farmers own their own land, but labor is communal, with villagers rotating their efforts through all the local plots. The landowner provides food and, at the end of the workday, hosts a party where everyone engages in joking, gossip and musicmaking. Little wonder that the Thai word, *ngan*, can mean both work and play. Barter is the traditional rural means of exchange, and although cash-poor, villagers rarely go hungry.

The Sino-Thai

The Chinese, mostly of Chiu Chao origin, arrived as laborers (and possibly traders) during 19th century industrialization and went on to become successful entrepreneurs. Thai society easily absorbs other ethnic groups; however, a pejorative term for the Chinese, *Jaek*, does exist.

It was during a period of anti-Chinese discrimination in the midst of World War II — when Thailand fell under Japanese sway — that a military prime minister changed the country's name from Siam (Khymer for "dark brown people") to Thailand (literally, "Land of the Free"). As the latter carries a subtle, anti-Chinese chauvinism, contemporary political progressives often prefer the older name. "Siam" still appears in the names of some newspapers, banks and companies, usually those owned by the government.

Today, Chinese-ethnic Thai are so assimilated into national life that there's little but their general prosperity to distinguish them from the rest of the population. *"The more Chinese blood, the more success"* is a Thai adage. Recently, however, that very prosperity has led to the country's official notion of ethnic homogeneity, of "Thai-ness" if you will, being challenged. Prominent Thai-Chinese have been asserting their unique identity by campaigning for public office in Chinese and by using such cultural symbols as the Chinese lion dance to attract fellow ethnic Chinese voters. In 1995, a former Bangkok governor temporarily changed his name from Chamlong Srimuang to Lu Jinhe ("River of Gold") in an effort to garner political support. Such tactics were unheard of a decade ago.

Authority and "Face"

The respect for authority instilled by Confucius on behalf of the Chinese imperial system still pervades Asia. Thais evince great deference toward occupational and social superiors, and hold the Thai royal family sacrosanct. Respect is accorded to age, experience and demonstrated wisdom. Loyalty is, however, to individuals rather than to institutions. Superiors are expected to repay deference with benevolence, personal interest and unfailing tactfulness.

A central underlying concept is "face" — dignity that's contingent on social relations (as opposed to pure self-respect). Aggressive competition is avoided, even in sports, as the will to win is an un-Buddhist craving and the loser would "lose face."

Occupational superiors are expected to "give face" to underlings (respect their dignity, praise their efforts) and to never openly criticize. If these expectations aren't met, and particularly if a Thai has been humiliated by public scolding, Thais may enlist others in the workplace to exact subtle sabotage or mass resignations, and they can turn brutally frank during their exit interviews.

With modernization, "getting big face" is increasingly coming to ride on such utterly un-Buddhist artifacts as Mercedes Benzes, cell phones, designer clothing and Rolex wristwatches.

How the Thai See Themselves

Although Thailand has suffered devastating invasions by its neighbors (especially Burma), , it's proud of the fact that it has never been colonized. Thai culture has existed without interruption for centuries — something that cannot be said about any other country in Asia.

Both homegrown and Western economists have dubbed Thailand "The Fifth Dragon" (the first four being Hong Kong, Korea, Singapore and Taiwan) for its rapid recent economic growth — five thousand new factories per year, financed largely by massive foreign investment. The country has the largest middle class, with the highest level of disposable income, in Asia.

The Thai see themselves as a spontaneous, adaptive people who take life as it comes and who treat each other with consideration. Life is to be enjoyed, not planned, and the goal is to maximize *sanuk* (fun). The most popular saying is *mai pen rai* — "no matter" or "never mind." What can't be cured must be ignored. The most admired personality embodies *jai yen* (a "cool heart"), never showing anger or distress. (However, that doesn't stop them from driving like madmen.) This reflects the Buddhist value of detachment from the ego's desires. Even pervasive crime and government corruption are tolerated with *mai pen rai*.

An increasing chasm between traditional Buddhist values and modern worldly values (power, prestige and wealth) is represented in a single word: *saksit*, meaning "amoral power." Many of Thailand's leading intellectuals feel that the renaming of Siam in 1938 (with a half-English word) was the first step toward creating a separation in the national character between traditional Theravada ideals and the depersonalized, thoroughly modern devotion to *saksit*.

Attitudes Toward Other Cultures

Farang, the Thai word for European-ethnic foreigners, is more descriptive than pejorative. For centuries, Thailand has been an Asian crossroads — trading with, absorbing influences from, and welcoming settlers from India, China, the Middle East, as well as Western nations. *Farang* can establish connections and friendships (at least superficial ones), assuming they adopt Thai manners. Learning Thai is, however, a prerequisite to full acceptance, because shared humor, including intricate wordplay, is a major element of social cohesion.

By astutely playing each would-be-invader against the others, the country managed to narrowly avoid European colonization during the 16th and the 19th centuries. Even today, Thais favor the United States over Britain and France because the U.S. never attempted colonization. The Thais' cosmopolitan attitude has played a notable role in their success as exporters of, initially, raw materials, and more recently, finished goods.

Beliefs About Westerners

Some common Thai views of Westerners are:

- They're big, hairy, clumsy and smell like meat.
- They're ill-mannered, barbaric hotheads.
- Westerners talk excessively about sex, yet they're puritanical when it comes to the act itself.
- Western women are enormous but pretty. They dress immodestly, talk too loudly and lose their tempers like the men.
- Regardless of specific nationalities, the men are aggressive "ugly Americans" who think that merely being Western and male makes them superior.
- While friendly on the surface, they care more about facts, figures and profits than about people and feelings.

After a week of eating wonderful Thai food, Westerners will cease to smell like meat. However, other issues are less easily overcome.

How Others View the Thai

In the past, if you mentioned Thailand, Westerners would think of Siamese cats, Siamese twins and *The King and I*. However, Siamese cats no longer much resemble their sturdier Asian ancestors and the most famous "Siamese" twins, Chang and Eng, were actually Chinese. And as for the King who became the subject of a Broadway musical — the real King Mongkhut (1851-1868) was, unlike his portrayal, a brilliant, progressive monarch who spoke several European languages, corresponded with Britain's Queen Victoria, knew enough astronomy to predict the course of a comet, and was a monk for 47 years prior to taking the throne.

Today, most Westerners think first of prostitution, then of AIDS, then peppery food, illegal drugs and political protests, followed by Bangkok's near-gridlocked traffic. And finally, they reflect that Thais are probably the most physically attractive people in the world. All these impressions are accurate. The food is spicy, the people are graceful, and prostitution and drugs, though illegal, are vast industries. (See Chapter 13.)

As for the 1973 and 1992 massacres of unarmed political activists and university students, the prime ministers who ordered them were summoned to conferences with King Bhumibol and immediately afterward resigned their posts and left the country. Nonetheless, the incidents fully restored the electorate's political cynicism, which had been temporarily weakened by brief periods of near-democracy.

In the realm of legitimate commerce, the West views Thailand as a source of cheap labor. Thai women, in particular, are known as hard and uncomplaining workers.

3 Cultural Stereotypes

Look Up to Westerners

Thais view Western culture as superior.

The fact is that for over a century, the Thai monarchy has actively fostered technical "modernization." Thais do admire Western creature comforts, technical know-how and consumer goods, but they "look up to" Westerners only in the literal sense, as they're somewhat shorter in height, on average. As noted in the previous chapter, Thais consider many aspects of Western culture to be ludicrous, even barbarous.

Everyone Is For Sale

Thais are the nicest people money can buy.

Money does completely control Thai politics, and it motivates the impoverished to work as criminals, prostitutes and sweatshop piece-workers. True, too, needy Thais may psychologically transcend any type of work, since Buddhism makes no value judgments about low-status professions, not even sex-work. However, Thais may subtly rebel against personal disrespect at any job, however well-paid, and even prostitutes (those not enslaved by brothels) turn down potential clients they dislike.

Many civil servants are indeed for sale. These government bureaucracy positions offer high prestige (now waning) and some petty power, but extremely low salaries. As in any nation, this is a perfect prescription for corruption.

Obsequious

Thais are fawningly attentive to the powerful.

Like most Asians, Thais adopt an extremely deferential posture toward superiors in a hierarchy, and often, wisely, toward those with the power to harm them. They may gush praise, but meanwhile their 'cool heart' approach helps them transcend workplace irritations. They never openly question decisions from above or bring problems to the attentions of 'higher-ups'. However, if they're sufficiently offended by what they consider to be mistreatment, they may seek subtle ways to undermine the offender.

Lazy Men

Thai women are workhorses, while the men slack off.

Thai women are indeed strong and hardworking. They labor in the rice paddies (or the office) all day, then cook for their families and keep house at night. Women will perhaps "put up with" more tedium, but both sexes pursue a unity between work and play that has no patience for routine, and both work to live, rather than the other way around.

(The Thai expression, *You're just like a water hyacinth*, means "You're good for nothing" — as water hyacinths grow wild and fast, clogging canals and waterways, but they have little utilitarian value.)

Regional Differences

Bangkok

Bangkok means "Village of the Olives." It's the center of Thai economic life, a city that is simultaneously nightmarish and alluring. Eighty percent of the country's jobs are here. "Bangkok today represents the dark side of the Asian economic miracle," Thomas L. Friedman recently wrote in *The New York Times*. "It is the story of what happens when a country imports free-market capitalism, but without the governing structures that go with it to regulate growth. More people per capita drive Mercedes Benzes in Bangkok than anywhere in the world [but they can't enjoy them] because they're always stuck in traffic."

Cars, motorbikes and *tuk-tuks* (pedicabs) crowd the streets between 7 A.M. and 7 P.M. The typical rush-hour commute rate is 5 km per hour (slow walking speed); most commuters consider cellular phones and portable potties indispensable automotive accessories. There's no subway system, no car-pool lanes, virtually no central planning, and massive pollution from exhaust. However, several mass-transportation projects are under construction, scheduled for completion by 1998.

Once, Bangkok was striated, like Venice, with navigable and fishable *khlongs* (canals). Developers filled in and built over most of them. However, "green belt" zoning regulations are now in place, and Bangkok is in the process of building more public parks.

Average income in Bangkok is as much as fifteen times higher than in outlying regions. As modern consumer goods gain cachet and the cash economy replaces village barter, large numbers of rural Thais migrate to the capital looking for work, straining the capital's infrastructure to the breaking point. (The government actively encourages the creation of business regions far from Bangkok.)

And yet, the charm of Bangkok goes deep. Elephants can sometimes be seen roaming the streets, foraging for food. Merit bowls in hand, Buddhist monks in saffron robes wait in line for buses beside office workers. Many of the temples are exquisite, dream-like, filled with offerings of jasmine, lotus flowers and incense, their roofs topped with golden "sky tassels." And the food can be spectacular. "A place... more ravishing than ravished," is how travel writer Pico Iyer describes it in *Video Night In Kathmandu.* "Lazily seductive... The most invigorating and accommodating city I had ever seen."

Nakhon Ratchasima (Korat)

Nakhon Ratchasima is a bustling, textile-manufacturing center known for its "Thai yuppies." In 1995, its population was approaching half a million and air pollution was already a problem. It's home to a considerable Khmer minority, as well as to some American GIs who were stationed here during the Vietnam war and never left. Nearby are some arresting Khmer ruins in the style of Angkor Wat.

Along with Chiang Mai, Korat may be the town of most interest to business travelers. Both cities are landlocked, so export goods must make their way slowly by rail to the coastal ports. Despite rapid development, the pace of life — and of production — is slower than in Bangkok, and, except at the newest plants, equipment may be aging.

Chiang Mai

Northern Chiang Mai ("New City") is a fascinating center of culture and crafts, including celadon, ceramics, silk, silver jewelry, gems, woodcarvings, leatherwork, dolls, lacquerware, "instant antiques," and the exquisite needlework of some twenty semi-nomadic hill tribes. The local women are renowned for their proud beauty (but be advised that the rate of HIV infection among Chiang Mai's B-girls was 70 percent in 1995 and rising).

A number of "hill tribe trekking" organizations are based here. In general, the tribes welcome trekkers (usually Westerners) — although no photos should be taken, especially of children, without asking permission, as some groups believe the camera steals the soul. Most of the tribes live at altitudes of 3,000 to 4,000 feet. Their life-styles are largely free of modern technology and elaborate possessions, and they prefer to keep it so. Typically, hill tribes grow, spin, weave, and dye their own cotton and then sew and embroider their garments in distinctive colors and patterns (tiny cross-stitches, red appliqué on indigo and white batik, silver studs and bells on black cloth, etc.).

Between tribes (some Tibeto-Burmese, others Khymer), customs vary as widely as costumes. While most hill tribes are illiterate, the Yao have their own form of script similar to Chinese. Sex roles and family structure range from adolescent "free love" and/or polygamy (among the Yao and Meo) to strict, lifelong monogamy (the Karen).

Opium poppies are a traditional cash crop. The tribal value system is such that opium-growing tribes often barter the drug in exchange for -- dried noodles! The Khmer tribes aren't involved with it, the Lisu sell it but use it only moderately (preferring betel nuts and home-made hooch), but many Meo males are addicts devoting their days to the pipe (while their wives farm, hunt, trap, cook, weave, sew, raise children, etc.).

The Southern Peninsula

Still the center of Thailand's batik mini-industry (fabrics handprinted with wax and dyes), this area is the site of a major tourist boom. Both Westerners and prosperous capital-dwellers take oceanfront vacations here.

Many pristine, isolated Thai beaches have been "discovered" and turned into pricey resorts. Phuket (once an Edenic site famed for inexpensive grilled fish dinners on the sand) is now home to "continental" dining and French tourists, who horrify the locals by sunbathing topless. (Only in fully Westernized resorts have the staffs become inured to seeing bikinis, tank tops and shorts. Islam is widely practiced in the south, but in a relatively tolerant form. Restrictions on food, alcohol and gambling are relaxed, and women are neither veiled nor subjected to genital mutilation. But even Buddhists are uncomforatble with near-nudity.)

However, it's still possible to truly "get away from it all." Krabi is famous for its numerous magnificent limestone islands, the island of Koh Phi Phi for its clear diving water. And after several weeks in Bangkok, your mental health may *require* a few days of surf and sand.

5 Government & Business

Stable, But Awash with Orchids

Thailand's government is peculiarly stable, given its perennial instability. In 1932, a coup by young, Western-educated officials forced the monarch to sign a constitution guaranteeing free elections. However, a frequently cited Thai saying is, "Corruption is as common as orchids." (Thai orchids are as common as dandelions.) Since 1932, military coups (mainly bloodless) have overthrown elected governments on grounds of "corruption" eighteen times. As of May, 1995, the longest-lasting civilian government endured three years.

Bangkok's elections are relatively clean, but the city controls only 40 of the parliament's 391 seats. In rural areas, "Godfather" financiers (including some drug lords) pay the high costs of campaigns for any office higher than the village headman, who is usually chosen by the voters' actual preference, rather than their pocketbooks. Marriages between prominent business and political families receive royal sponsorship. Direct bribes and pork barrels (government projects or appropriations yielding rich patronage) rule.

Radio and television stations are controlled by the government and the military. *Mong Tang Moom* ("Different Perspectives"), a popular, outspoken current affairs TV show, was forced off the air in February 1996 for its insistence on raising questions about political hanky-panky.

A Vertical Hierarchy

In the mid 1980s, foreign investors flocked to Thailand to take advantage of its cheap, unregulated labor. Now, with those same investors setting up shop in China and Vietnam, the government is eager for industrial development. Because official policies encourage free trade with minimal government interference, Thailand's current economy is often compared to the "robber baron" era of the West.

Seven agencies, including the government-owned Bank of Thailand, are charged with devising and executing economic policy. One agency, the Industrial Committee, has the Herculean task of coordinating the other six, which have varying and often-contradictory agendas. Unfortunately, the Thai organizational model is a vertical hierarchy, with little horizontal contact between agencies or between separate functions within the same agency. Functions are in fact fiefdoms, and obtaining approval from one agency, branch or department doesn't guarantee approval by the others. Furthermore, petty officials often deliberately create obstacles in order to exercise power or encourage bribes.

The Board of Investment handles 80 percent of direct foreign investments. Emerging industries that seem to hold the greatest promise for foreign monies include waste treatment, water purification, energy conservation, auto parts, electronics, machine-tooling, plastic molding and engineering. Multinational corporations that wish to qualify for government incentives must spend a minimum of US$400,000 to establish a regional headquarters and relocate at least 50 employees.

Both government and commercial bureaucracies include a *saraban*, a department charged with precisely tracking the flow of paperwork up and down the protracted chain of command. Needless to say, progress is exasperatingly slow, but without the *saraban*, documents are guaranteed to disappear forever inside the bureaucratic labyrinth.

The Government's Business Agenda

As noted earlier, the government grants special concessions (tax holidays of up to eight years, export subsidies, investment guarantees, VAT exemptions) to enterprises in "zone three" — everywhere but Bangkok and its surrounding areas. Projects having the greatest chance of government approval are non-polluting industries that make use of local materials and labor and that have Thai-majority ownership.

Thailand requires that many new enterprises (including rice farming, real estate, mining, law, architecture and construction) be at least 51 percent Thai-owned. However, foreigners often manage to circumvent this by enlisting investment by a bank, or by numerous inactive shareholders.

The country is eager to import modern technology, but this often conflicts with the desire for a favorable trade balance. Hence, a thicket of obscure and oft-contradictory regulations surrounds the import field. Taxes are high, multiple, and complicated. Foreign import firms can't succeed without a Thai lawyer and Thai accountant to hack a path through the bureaucratic maze.

As for exports, upper-echelon officials are responsible for coordinating local industrial production with other nations' import quotas. Many quotas go to firms partly owned by the government or by the officials themselves, or are given in return for favors or gratuities. Foreign concerns hoping to export directly from Thai factories usually choose business partners who already possess quota licenses.

Tea Money

"Tea money" is a common method of "greasing the wheels" of business in Asia. Subtle and indirect, it goes by many names — including research charges, commissions and technical fees.

Until fairly recently, Thai government decisions were made slowly and often arbitrarily. The bureaucracy was a glutton for paperwork, and any low-level bureaucrat could stop a business cold (albeit with perfect grace and politeness). Merely bringing in samples to show Thai counterparts in an import venture involved multiple, detailed inventories and reports. Often, businesses were relieved to dispense "tea money" in order to expedite things.

However, this practice is no longer as prevalent as it once was. For the most part, "tea money" only changes hands between Thais, not between Thais and non-Thais. And such exchanges are virtually nonexistent in the financial services sector (banking, securities, accounting, etc.). Still, in some cases, it may advantageous to hire a local agent to help you navigate. Be aware that when it comes to public sector contracts, the Counter Corruption Commission is fairly diligent about seeking out unwary public servants (and their books) for scrutiny.

6 The Work Environment

Thailand is a developing country, an Asian country and a tropical country. To Westerners, the work environment can seem like a voyage through both time and space, with its mingling of courtly Asian paternalism, feudal hierarchy, neo-Dickensian work relations (for both good and ill), Industrial Revolution machinery and modern computer equipment. Still, it's easier to conduct business here than in China, for example, as the Thai are more open and less hidebound.

Accept, But Don't Excel

The Buddhist concept of *karma* states that you're born to a certain role in life which you must enjoy (or endure) as best you can. If your current life's *karma* sends you to the brothel or the sweatshop, serenely accepting and bearing it will improve your *karma* for the next life. But striving to excel indicates non-acceptance of your *karma*, as well as a hungry ego. As a result, many Thai work all their lives for one company, more interested in warm relationships and interesting tasks than in advancement. (The Thai word for "work," *ngam*, also means festival and communality.)

"Thai yuppie" managers who enthusiastically pursue wealth and power often suffer a deep ambivalence over their adoption of such chilly, *karma*-wrecking values. During the last five years, however, with growing influence from the West and with many affluent young Thais returning home with finance, insurance, real estate, management and service industry degrees from abroad, this non-competitive approach has been rapidly going by the wayside.

Benignly Paternal vs. "Western"

Traditionally, the Thai workplace functioned like an extended family led by a wise and forgiving father who cared for all his children's welfare equally. Only the most extreme misconduct merited disinheritance. Firings were considered a great "loss of face" for both the manager and the employee. Frequently, numerous members of a single family worked for the same firm, which lent a certain leverage, as well as comfort. If one family member was sufficiently offended (for instance, by an overt demotion), the whole family was likely to quit.

Bosses were expected to evince personal interest in employees. Superiors routinely devoted time to socializing outside the office with subordinates and their families at, for instance, birthdays. (The head of the company was likely to attend major personal celebrations, such as marriages.) Managers who failed to manifest personal concern and vast tact sometimes found themselves subtly sabotaged, as subordinates considered a personal bond to be broken and an unspoken contract violated. Thais were appalled by the Western approach wherein managers exhibited hearty, egalitarian friendliness but actually viewed employees as interchangeable cogs. (To be seen as a mere cog is the *ultimate* loss of face.)

Status was determined by position, age and, to some extent, seniority. Wisdom, another status-giver, was measured not only by intelligent deci-sion-making and effectiveness, but also by having harmonious relations up and down the hierarchy.

The Western habit of periodic employee evalu-ations — frank written and oral discussion of an individual's performance — was unheard of. Gen-erally speaking, workers were expected to simply do the best they could. If a worker failed grossly to meet even these gentle expectations, he or she was given a lower position with a more grandiose title, such as "Prince of the Copy Machine."

Even at the management level, where expecta-tions are somewhat higher, direct performance criti-cism was taboo. Instead, a superior was likely to frame the issue as a *group* problem, or to discuss it hypothetically, or metaphorically, using proverbs and adages. In this way, the idea of what was expected was conveyed without anyone losing face.

There was virtually no horizontal mesh and lit-tle horizontal communication or teamwork. Middle managers were anything but eager to make major decisions or accept responsibility. A senior official might say that he had to check with someone at a higher level, even if no such person existed, in order to "save face" and avoid confrontation. The top boss alone was supposed to know all aspects of a company's operations.

"Staff development" was largely absent. Often, blue-collar workers were only minimally trained and were expected to develop skills by emulating others on the job. Even when a new skill was widely required, instruction often consisted of example-oriented spot training rather than formal group instruction. This dearth of technical skills (plus the obsolete machinery at many sites), far more than the non-competitive workplace ethos, contributed to the country's relatively low per-worker productivity. Nonetheless, Thai products were usually of sufficient quality to compete with those of other Asian nations.

All that having been said, the past decade has brought about rapid change and major new opportunities for Western-style management. Most university students come from "good" urban families who, until very recently, believed that the purpose of education was to create well-rounded individuals, rather than careers. As a result, most students gravitated to liberal arts.

Today, the vast majority of the young Thais being groomed to take over large Thai companies (usually owned by their parents or families) obtain their business degrees from MIT, Harvard, USC and other U.S.-based universities. And more and more non-Asian businesses are establishing branches or joint partnerships in Thailand. The blending of East and West is happening as never before, and the trend is destined to continue.

Code of Silence

Traditionally, Thais have a deep distaste for conveying bad news. It's not only tactless, but it might have ill consequences. In extremely rare cases, workers may present a group petition — a situation that indicates true desperation. The combination of keeping bad news a secret and assuming it will be beneficial to do so is typically Thai.

(During World War II, when Thailand (under Japanese sway) declared war on the U.S., the Thai ambassador in Washington refused to pass on the message. As a result, America never knew about its new "enemy," and after the war, Thailand seamlessly resumed excellent relations with the U.S.)

Until very recently, out of both personal consideration for superiors and perhaps anxiety about the consequences, subordinates in the workplace were loathe to "trouble" higher-ups with any bad news. In the face of this code of silence, the boss was often ignorant of the most severe problems within his operation. However, with the aforementioned influx of Western management techniques, this reticence is quickly disappearing.

Village in the Office

Thailand remains a rural culture at heart. The Thai genius for *sanuk* (fun) transforms even the drudgery of rice-farming into a pleasurable social experience. The goal is to enjoy life, at work as well as during leisure. Hence, white collar employees may seem less "serious" about their tasks than their Western counterparts. However, in Bangkok, workers put in an average of forty hours a week.

The Growing Cachet of Money

Thais expect time off from work to run errands and fulfill social commitments, for special occasions and personal crises, and time on the job for socializing with colleagues. But here too, things are changing, especially within Bangkok business circles.

In the past, an interest in money (as in careers) was considered unfit for people of good families. But today, the middle class has discovered the lure of Western consumerism and is becoming more overtly financially aggressive. More money is becoming equated with more *sanuk*.

The Working Class: Charles Dickens Redux

Work is rarely fun for the working class. Often, they're crowded into brutally hot factories, toiling away at obsolete machines in polluted environments. Although the government sets minimum standards for wages and conditions, these are often violated, especially in plants with mass employment of women. Factory workdays may run to twelve hours — with no overtime rates or even regular bathroom breaks. A few years ago, a fire in a doll factory killed hundreds of women and children, a replay of New York's infamous Triangle Shirtwaist Factory fire of 1911. The common factor between the two tragedies was that the women, working for a pittance, were locked inside the factories throughout the work day.

While labor unions are legal, membership remains minuscule. The concepts of opposition between classes and overt struggle are alien to a communitarian culture that stresses interpersonal harmony.

As a result of the inflation affecting all sectors of the economy and increasing opportunities for education (and hence middle-class occupations), Thai factory wages have, on average, increased rapidly since 1990. As a result, many foreign-owned factories have relocated to Indonesia, Vietnam and China.

7 Women in Business

Traditional Roles

Traditional Thai culture pays lip service to the concept of women as meek, obedient wives, and women may, in fact, exhibit a soft-spoken graciousness. But Thai culture is matriarchal, and considerably more egalitarian than most in Asia.

Eight hundred years ago, Thailand was the Asian equivalent of "the Wild West," and women's vital role in settling the territory produced an enduring legacy of respect. *Women are the hind legs of the elephant* goes an old Thai adage. Women have been active traders for centuries, and in many areas of the country they've controlled the family budget (especially true at the lower economic levels).

Suffrage (for both sexes) arrived with the Thai Constitution in 1932. Women can own land, and in some areas, they gain ownership of their husband's property when they wed. Polygamy continues to exist; *mia noi* (minor wives) — both a Chinese and Muslim tradition — are common and winked at by the law. However, a woman can't initiate divorce on the grounds of adultery (a husband can).

Thailand's queen plays an active role in both social and developmental issues — supporting traditional craft industries and touring with her husband, talking one-on-one with people in various regions. Her mother-in-law, the Princess Mother, was active in bringing medical care to rural areas.

Changing Trends

Lower-class women have long worked in the mills and factories, sometimes suffering worse wage and safety conditions than men. Within the more comfortable classes, business was traditionally considered too aggressive an enterprise for the well-bred of either sex. Educated women entered civil service, earning modest salaries but high prestige and security. However, the civil service's very firm "glass ceiling" has led many talented women into the private sector.

Women now constitute roughly half the university student population. They run major companies, manage most urban real estate, and are often hired as Market Managers in export companies. Thailand's largest hotel chain (the Dusit Tani) and Thailand's largest steel mill (Sahaviriya City Public Co., Ltd.) are both chaired by women. Some have even become "tycoons." However, they rarely present themselves in the mode of stereotyped Western "career" women, choosing instead to maintain a highly feminine mien.

Strategies for Foreign Businesswomen

Visiting businesswomen will best fulfill their objectives if they adapt to Thai manners — which require both sexes to behave in a fashion the West calls "ladylike." Women, in particular, should speak in quiet voices, patiently allow others to speak without interruption, and above all avoid displaying anger. (Since Thai of both sexes take care to appear unassertive, they're liable to be appalled by a show of open aggression by a *farang* woman.) Your counterparts will find you charming if you demonstrate personal (but not sexual) interest in their lives as well as in their business activities. Be prepared, however, to gently parry questions that you may find over-personal ("Who's caring for your children while you're here?"). These aren't rudely intended. When dealing with government bureaucracies, a woman may actually have an advantage, *if* she can evince deep, dignified sorrow, rather than anger, at the inevitable frustrations.

Preparing for a Visit

Before you begin your trip, make sure that your group is well-briefed in Thai business etiquette. Thais consider Western "give and take" brutal, and all the more embarrassing if a woman's ideas are subject to public interruption or contradiction. However, Thais will not be surprised or made uncomfortable by a woman team leader.

Foreign businesswomen are welcomed at most social-business lunches and dinners. Thai women managers (at least the younger ones) drink alcohol moderately at these functions. However, women are unlikely to be invited to Patpong bars or clubs (see Chapter 20, "What Passes for a Nightclub") by their male associates after dinner. This will make it somewhat more difficult for them to form the personal relationships that are the basis of most of the country's business.

8   Making Connections

Choosing suitable business partners can be a mysterious process. Due to vast spatial and cultural distances, such relationships will have to be based on near-absolute mutual trust. Expect to make several visits over many months before either you or your potential Thai colleague come to a decision. Those involved in import/export should establish a line of credit at a Thai bank even before beginning to make contacts in the country. This will be a prerequisite to obtaining commitments for meetings with Thai companies.

Some Thais may be more likely to trust a *farang* than a fellow Thai. For all the gracelessness of the *farangs'* direct approach to business, many Thai believe that same directness is a sign of uncorrupt business ethics.

Unless you're conducting business in a major city, your counterparts may be unfamiliar with your company (regardless of how large and reputable it is). As one Western businessman put it, "For many Thais, Marcie's Boutique and Macy's New York are the same." Only the larger Thai companies routinely make an advance effort to investigate a *farang* company's size or soundness, so representatives of a start-up are often treated much the same as those of a giant corporation — to the former's advantage and the latter's annoyance. If yours is a large company courting a known and specific Thai company, consider inviting your counterpart to your country for a series of preliminary meetings early on.

Methods of Approach

Ask friends or colleagues with Thai business connections to provide letters of introduction and/or a list of contacts. Or hire a local independent agent or facilitator — preferably one who speaks Thai and who has already established relationships — to make all initial contacts for you. (You may find such an agent through your country's Thailand-based government agencies, business associations, trade organizations or chambers of commerce, or through international lawyers, accounting firms, or Thai or international banks.) If yours is a small company, consider locating and joining forces with a potential licensee, distributor, or joint venture partner. If you're a small import/export firm, consider seeking out a small Thai company that functions as a mirror-image of your own (e.g., exporting, if your intention is to import).

Advance Preparations

Thai companies will often respond to "cold calls" from afar, especially if you're calling at the recommendation of someone of influence (a bank president, for example). Send a fact-sheet packed with information about what your company does and whom you do business with — both in Thailand, your native country and elsewhere. Be sure to note which Thai bank and customs broker you use.

Thais will take this information very seriously. When arranging for an appointment with a large company, contact them a month or two in advance.

Organize your time before you go. Schedule in advance as many meetings as you can, and, if appropriate, arrange to have your counterparts bring samples of their export product to the initial meeting. At the start of your correspondence, offer to wire money ahead to pay for the samples, upon receipt of an invoice. Even if the company refuses to accept payment, the offer will be taken as a mark of seriousness. A company's ability to comply with this procedure is an indication of its overall ability to perform.

Preparing a Schedule

The trip to Thailand takes a minimum of 17 hours from California, New York City or London, with at least one change of planes. Expect to suffer severe jet lag and culture shock. The Thai are justly proud of their cultural heritage, so if you're new to the country, try to schedule in an extra few days for sight-seeing. Flexibility is key.

Be aware that if you meet your counterparts at their offices, near-gridlocked traffic and the chance of getting lost en route will affect your schedule. It's best to pick a hotel as close as possible to your appointments. When taking taxis in Bangkok, have the address of your destinations, and instructions for getting there, written down in Thai. And consider bringing along a detailed map. Many drivers know only the main streets. If you have a number of appointments in the same day, consider hiring a car and driver.

An alternative is to use your hotel for appointments — a two-hour meeting at 10 A.M., a two-hour business lunch at 1 P.M., a brief 4 P.M. coffee meeting (to give you an excuse to end the lunch meeting), and, for your most important contact, a dinner starting at 7 P.M. Thais rarely object to spending a few hours in a luxury hotel. Schedule visits to factories (in the outlying suburbs) for the weekend, when traffic subsides somewhat.

Assembling a Team

Your team should include at least one person who is thoroughly familiar with doing business in Thailand, and another who is highly knowledgeable about the import/export business and/or your specific industry or business.

Consider working with a fully bilingual Thai who resides in your own country, someone who can ensure that your counterparts fully understand the terms being negotiated. However, in Bangkok and other big cities, this may be unnecessary, as business will probably be conducted in English.

The Vital Choice of a Hotel

An excellent hotel lends status, and choosing one that caters to business rather than tourism will be taken as an indication of earnestness. Try to choose one relatively close to the offices of your counterparts. Any of the four (as of 1995) business-oriented four-star hotels on Sukumvit Road will probably be the most convenient. These provide, at minimum, meeting rooms, trade reference guides, fax machines, and help in securing business services.

Once you've established a solid relationship with Thai counterparts, it will be acceptable (and amusing) to ask them to book you a hotel "at Thai people rates" (if yours is a small firm). You will, of course, be indebted for the favor, which you can repay by hosting a dinner or giving a special gift.

SPEAK MODESTLY

INTERACT PERSONALLY

KEEP A "COOL HEART"

RELATIONSHIPS FIRST

9 Strategies for Success

For *farangs*, successful business relationships require striking a fine balance between local expectations (of personal relationships and *sanuk*) and Western requirements for predictable performance. If you attempt to conduct your business by Thai rules, you'll risk taking on the disorders of a tropical country in the throes of development. The secret is to understand Thailand's business culture and to integrate it with your own.

Most important of all: Listen to what your Thai counterparts want, treat them as you wish to be treated (with forthrightness, honesty and integrity), and be sure to ask questions.

12 Keys to Business Success

1. Relationships first

That personal relationships are essential to business can't be overemphasized. Expect to make many trips in order to establish them, and allow ample time for trust to develop. Don't expect to leave with a signed contract after your first meeting, or even after your third trip.

Be aware that Thais are skeptical about the ability

of many Westerners to implement their promises. Experience has taught them that Americans (in particular) expect to get *paid* to learn how to conduct business in their country, that they want money up front, and that they expect to "make a quick killing and get out fast." Such short-term vision is antithetical to the Thai way. It's essential to understand the Thai perspective on your project and to keep in mind what they will get out of it.

2.   Keep a "cool heart"

Avoid open demonstrations of impatience, anger or frustration — such as sighing, watch-checking or interrupting. Displays of temper are considered spiritually ugly and will lose you respect. (However, Thais occasionally unleash a repressed fury at apparently minor or unintended insults that cause them to "lose face" — as revealed by a murder rate equivalent to that of Washington, DC.)

Another Thai concept is *krieng jai* ("contraction of the heart"). Generally speaking, it means that self-interest and personal desires should be held in check, in order to keep others from feeling uncomfortable.

3.   Adapt to Thai culture

Many Thai will refuse to continue a business relationship with an outsider who has caused them to "lose face." Foreigners must learn to smile and express themselves with tact. Learning at least a few words in Thai, difficult as it is, will work to your advantage. (On occasion, new ventures will not proceed until after an astrologer has been consulted to ascertain which times are most auspicious or until your Thai counterpart has visited a local *wat* to pray for guidance.)

4.   Aim high, but be friendly with lower ranks

Approach your counterparts at the highest organizational level possible. The head of the Thai company may or may not meet with you initially (it will depend, in part, on who made the introduction and on how senior you are within your organization), but no decision will be made without his or her direct involvement. However, your warmest and most important relationships will usually be with those of a lower rank.

5. Feelings are facts

Logical argument, in and of itself, will get you nowhere. Personal rapport will make the difference between a possibility and a partnership. Slighting anyone in an organization can be taken as a slight to all. Business relationships that traverse vast geographic and cultural distances require great mutual trust. Listen to your intuition about prospective counterparts. The Thai will be listening to theirs.

6. Present a united front

Don't refer to the failures of any colleagues (from the Thai group or your own), even if they aren't present. And don't vent internal disagreements in front of your Thai counterparts. Thais view these behaviors as antithetical to group harmony. Great cultural emphasis is placed on individuals *not* speaking out. However, after an initial rapport has been established, brainstorming with the other side is quite acceptable.

7. Don't Try to Be Thai

Westerners should scrupulously follow all the requisites of politeness (see Chapter 18) to avoid offending. However, being an outsider can sometimes work in your favor. One wily *farang* businessman, a long-time resident in Thailand, has adapted the strategy of speaking Thai in social interactions, but only English at business meetings. In this way, he makes it known that he expects his counterparts' performance to conform to Western requisites of promptness and precision. While Westerners can never hope to be mistaken for Thais, they *can* be accepted as honorable *farang* business partners, and even as *farang* friends.

8. Be clear at the beginning and at completion

When setting up meetings, directly state your basic requirements (such as expecting to see samples, evidence of financial responsibility, etc.). Be even more explicit in the final stages of discussion — lay out all your expectations, write them into your contract, and then go over them orally, point by point. Don't let details slide, hoping for the best.

9. Interact personally, but state doubts impersonally

After all your efforts to build personal relationships, you may still endanger them during the difficult task of finalizing a deal. Clearly declaring your expectations may sometimes imply unflattering doubts about your Thai counterparts' willingness or ability to perform. (If you say, "We won't accept substitute goods," it implies that inferior products may be substituted.) Present your requirements as impersonal needs, e.g., "Our lawyers insist that...." Also, try to avoid questions like "Is Mr. X someone I can trust?" or "What do you think of our products?" Such directness puts the other person on the spot.

10. Invite bad news

Once you've sealed a relationship, your open insistence on receiving unvarnished information may relieve your counterparts of their cultural inhibition against conveying it. One successful American businessman sent the following fax to his ominously-silent Thai partners: *Bad news is better than no news.* Their return fax was a veritable outpouring of woes. He had, essentially, given them permission to tell him what he needed to learn, and they behaved as though he'd released them from a prison of discretion.

11. Be ready for 'Murphy's Law'

Try to anticipate all the things that can possibly go wrong — because they will — and address these concerns one by one. And know that there'll be other glitches and setbacks you probably *won't* be able to anticipate. Allow twice as long for global transactions as you would for transactions within your own country.

12. Tap into the Middle Class

In the past, foreign investors viewed Thailand as a place to manufacture items for export. But more and more, investors are working to create a consumer market *within* Thailand's burgeoning middle class. A few success stories:

- Frito-Lay has created a demand for its potato chips (including barbecue-flavored ones) through local TV commercials, by giving farmers special seeds, and by training them in soil monitoring and equipment usage.

- Citicorp's Citibank has garnered 40 percent of Thailand's credit card market.

- Tower Records opened a huge franchise in Bangkok in early 1995, selling Thai CDs along with Western jazz and rock n' roll albums.

- Other recent Western arrivals in Bangkok include Planet Hollywood, a Hard Rock Cafe, and a Giorgio Armani boutique.

- In 1986, the total number of automobiles sold nationwide was under 50,000. A decade later, the number had risen tenfold. It's predicted that by the year 2000, Thailand will be the third-largest auto producer in East Asia.

- Despite the traditional Asian aversion to dairy products, Thailand is now home to 68 Pizza Hut outlets and 45 Swenson's ice cream shops.

Time

"Thai Time"

In Thailand, the concept of time remains fundamentally attached to the unhurried, repetitive framework of tropical agriculture, where there's no looming 'first frost date' to make the farmer frantic. Thai time is also defined by Buddhist reincarnation, the endless turning of the Wheel of Life. Time is fluid, slow and cyclical, rather than linear, swift and absolute. What isn't completed today can be completed tomorrow, or next week. Westerners shouldn't confuse a lack of punctuality, or what they consider to be "slowness," with laziness. Be aware, however, that this very traditional approach no longer applies in Bangkok business circles.

Deadlines: Then & Now

Traditionally, Thais were willing to work hard when a project was engaging and there was an obvious, immediate benefit. However, they weren't greatly attracted by promises of later rewards. Schedules, short-term plans, inventories, spreadsheets, payrolls and balance sheets were looked on as unendurably petty and boring.

This quarter's profits were considered a minor matter compared to a company's long-term goals, reputation and prosperity. And there was always time at work to socialize with peers, friends, and family members. Precipitous decisions were believed to create trouble later on, and deadlines were disdainfully referred to as *mother's lists*.

But as previously noted, since about 1992, Thailand has been rapidly adopting a more "Western" approach. Today, foreign businesspeople are likely to be dealing directly with senior people, and agreements (including specific deadlines) will be honored.

Appointments

Whatever the means of transportation, getting around Bangkok is slow and unpleasant. And nobody wants to spend hours inhaling gasoline fumes on a gamble that the person they want to see *may* be available. Make your appointments in advance, and reconfirm them the day before.

Be on time if possible; it's expected of Western businesspeople. Your Thai counterparts are likely to be a few minutes late, especially if they're meeting away from their work sites and must negotiate traffic. If you're going to see them, schedule your meetings for after the morning rush (after about 10 A.M.), and allow additional time to cope with congestion and the chance that your taxi may get lost.

11 Business Meetings

Arranging the Meeting

Although Thais love spontaneity, it's advisable to arrange initial meetings before you leave your home country. This will serve to maximize your time with companies that are actively interested in your project. You may be able to set up meetings after you arrive in Thailand (especially with smaller companies), but it's unwise to gamble on it. Be sure, though, to leave some room in your schedule for spontaneous social/business engagements, which will arise as people get to know you.

The level of the managers who'll meet with you will depend on the nature of your company, the level of your introduction, and the size of the Thai company in question (not on the size of yours). If you and your project seem acceptable, you'll move up to meeting mid- and upper-level managers. As you progress toward a contract, your dealings will usually be with the heads of those departments that will actually execute your undertaking. Since these managers will supervise the actual work on your project, they're the people best able to assess their sections' capacity to handle the tasks. Their recommendations will consider both their view of you and their tacit judgments about their own departments.

The ultimate decision will be delegated to the topmost level, but it will be based on messages from below. Then, too, every hour you spend with functional management personnel is time spent building rapport in a culture where relationships are the ultimate key not only to a contract, but also to a project's success.

If your enterprise involves opening a new manufacturing facility, you may have to schedule numerous appointments to meet or eat with various officials from every government bureau that can have any possible regulatory interest in your enterprise.

Preparing for the First Meeting

Make sure that all team members have been briefed in basic Thai etiquette (see Chapter 18). Although Thais are relaxed about business, they are sensitive about violations of their unique protocol.

Before an initial meeting with any company, mail or fax a rank-ordered list of all your team members' names and titles, with brief biographical information (degrees, credentials, special accomplishments) for each of them, and a slightly longer biography of the team leader. In addition, outline the project you're proposing, so that your Thai counterparts will have time to decide whether it's appropriate for them, and to assign the most appropriate persons to meet with you. Your counterparts will probably be fluent in English.

Presenting Your Business

Before and during your visit, make the nature of your business clear. Thais are rarely familiar with *farang* companies that don't already have Thai branches, and their own companies rarely engage in corporate public relations activities. Questions about your business will usually be brought up casually and framed obliquely at the exploratory 'let's do lunch' meetings.

Be ready, at a formal meeting, to provide letters of recommendation from banks, officials, and/or mutual business acquaintances, or equivalent proofs of reputability. And ask to see the equivalent from the companies *you're* interviewing. However, such precautions won't be necessary if you've had the proper introductions.

Consider putting together a small presentation kit, printed on good stock, preferably with a Thai translation. Include a company brochure and a brief overview that lists the names and ranks of top executives, as well as a summary of the company's philosophy, values, "mission statement" and accomplishments. Don't force these kits on your counterparts, but feel free to distribute them at the end of the first meeting or after lunch. A corporation can enhance its presentation by making a short video documentary showing the facilities, and having staffers give information about company methods, accomplishments and products. (In this case, bring a VCR, too, as Thailand's videotape equipment isn't compatible with VHS formats).

Business Card Protocol

Most business meetings will begin with an exchange of business cards. (If need be, you can have cards printed up locally. At first class hotels, ask your hotel desk clerk for assistance.) While there's no special ritual attached to the act, your card should be of good quality on heavy stock (Thais have a keen esthetic sense and an even keener eye for status) and should include as much information as possible. Printing the reverse side with a Thai translation isn't essential; most Thais recognize that it serves as a rough guide to pronunciation, at best.

When others give you their cards, look briefly at each one before putting it away. Treat the cards with respect (don't use them for jotting down notes or for cleaning your nails), and take them with you when the meeting ends — regardless of your decision about doing business with the people who presented them. It's insulting to discard them in the giver's presence.

Thai Meetings and Meeting Thais

Begin initial meetings with introductions, handshakes, and exchanges of business cards (see Chapter 14).

During the early stages (and later stages, too), business may sometimes seem more like socializing. Often, the initial meetings will consist of informal lunches during which business is barely discussed. Don't force the talk toward your project.

However, when presenting your proposal to higher levels of management, the team leader should set forth the overall picture in some detail. Each team member must thoroughly understand his or her own aspect of your business. However new or small your company may be, it's essential to include team members who can speak expertly on issues of finance and (if in import/export projects), shipping.

When making a presentation to a group, speak slowly and clearly, but not over-loudly. Thais are usually familiar with spoken English (including slang), but they may still need time to mentally translate. Avoid long monologues. The Thai already feel that Westerners talk too much. If an older person is present, treat him with deference, regardless of his official rank.

Asking for your listeners' questions is worth trying. However, never ask Thais blunt questions about their opinions (e.g., "What do you think of our product?"). This is considered to be so rude that they'll probably just laugh. As rapport develops (or fails to), you'll be able to surmise their opinions.

Assigning Meeting Times

The specific hour and the amount of time you schedule for each meeting should be guided by the stage of negotiations you've reached, as well as by the company's relative importance to your project. As noted earlier, inducing your Thai contacts to meet at your hotel (instead of having to travel to their offices) will increase your efficiency, not to mention your physical comfort.

From the Thai side, meetings will be scheduled according to the urgency of the deal in question. Generally speaking, however, lunchtime meetings (1 – 3 P.M.) are used for ice-breaking and relationship-building in duos or small groups. Don't overcrowd lunches or coffee dates with a large team. Note that restaurant checks are never split; the inviter is usually the host.

More formal presentation meetings, as well as those working out details of a deal, are typically held at 10 A.M. (2 P.M. on days with no lunch dates). The whole team should probably be present. End afternoon meetings before 4 P.M., as by then, your counterparts will be eager to leave work.

The most important meeting of the day is the three-hour dinner starting at 7 P.M. (usually followed by nightclubbing). If your schedule is crowded, reserve this slot for actively courting middle or higher-up managers of a good company — or politicians and officials, if your project will require official permits. On subsequent trips, your schedule will grow more complex as you hold more meetings of varying lengths, with varying levels of seriousness.

Keep in mind that managers who haven't met you may not want to give up their free time for an unknown. You may first have to prove that spending time with you will be *sanuk* — fun. Dinner meetings are usually small, attended by only the leaders or central members of each team. Just before or after a contract is signed, the dinner group may expand to a dozen-plus people, often including at least one politician friend of the Thai company's top manager or owner.

Spouses may be invited to smaller dinner meetings, but be aware that Thai wives generally decline invitations to larger dinners. As a rule of thumb, women should bring their spouses only if their male counterparts bring their wives. If in doubt, check with your host.

 # 12 Negotiating with the Thai

Many meetings and social occasions are actually informal negotiation sessions. Eventually, though, you will have to negotiate more formally. The Thai use negotiating sessions primarily to gather information about your business and your project. There will be many such sessions, until gradually they'll feel that they've obtained a complete picture of you, and you of them. But the decisions will be made elsewhere, and slowly, until finally a detailed contract or agreement is drawn up.

Think in Years, Not Fiscal Quarters

Before you begin serious negotiations, arrange with your group to present a united front. Your team may want to devise some subtle visual signal or verbal code each member can use to signify an 'alert' or a disagreement that needs to be discussed later, out of the Thais' presence. Thais are accustomed to taking several meetings before any decision is reached, so there's no need to hurry your own decisions while your team members still have issues to discuss.

Usually, negotiating sessions begin with friendly small talk, as those present remove their jackets (if they're wearing them) and try to get comfortable.

It's important to recognize that your motives and Thai motives are likely to differ. Thais are ruled less by considerations of their stock exchange (which has matured considerably in the last decade) than by considerations of foreign exchange, less by shareholder's hopes than by the hope of shared skills and technologies. They may care less for quick profits than for quality goods, reliable supplies, obtaining technical aid or training, and/or conforming to Thai government regulations and policies. Thais will often be much more patient about awaiting profits than Western companies. Unless they're among the new breed of "Thai yuppies," they may be thinking ahead by years, not fiscal quarters.

Beware of Perceived Slights

The negotiating sessions are also relationship-building sessions. You may lose points, or the whole agreement, if anyone in the Thai group feels you've shown him disrespect. Foreign business representatives have been appalled to find promising relationships broken off in the final stages, and at the highest level of the Thai group, because a "minor" member of the Thai team perceived a slight or "loss of face." If one team member feels insulted, all may withdraw.

If the Thais start making excuses, suddenly "forget" their English, or (if top-level) say they need to consult a (mythical) higher level for a decision, this probably means that things aren't proceeding in your favor.

Linguistic Pitfalls Can Hinder — or Help

Between any two languages, there's always the danger of misunderstanding. This familiar dilemma can harm you, but it can also provide a convenient route out of the tact-versus-directness problem. Many successful Western negotiators "blame" their directness on the well-known perils of translation. You can, as you go through your points of agreement, ask your Thai counterparts to confirm, in both English and Thai, their under-standing of each detail agreed to. (This is why an ideal team should include a bilingual Thai who's a long-term resident of your own country.) In your "clarifications," you can impersonally but explicitly pin down issues that have proved elusive.

If negotiations grow tense and start to bog down, the Thais will probably make a few jokes or change the subject. Follow along and return to the sticking point later, or at another meeting. Thais can't countenance open arguments. If your natural reaction to tensions is to yell or vent — don't. Remember Soviet premier Nikita Khrushchev pounding his shoe on the table at the United Nations? Had he been in Thailand, he would prob-ably have been fined for fatal boorishness and deported on the next scow to Vladivostok.

Confidentiality = Saving Face

Confidentiality is important within the Thai framework. Making concessions or admitting prob-lems can make a person or a whole company lose face, with potential damage to local dealings. Often a one-to-one negotiating session will be held (perhaps disguised as a dinner) to tacitly set conditions and explore compromises. It's understood that you shouldn't publicize these negotiations at the formal sessions or outside of your group. Neither should you publicly disclose details of your final agreement.

White Elephants & Patent Pirates

White elephants are the privileged pets of Thai royalty and are considered to be sacred. They're enormously expensive to maintain, requiring a staff of twenty to massage and bathe them, rub them with cream (to diminish wrinkles), dust their hides with rice powder, mascara their eyelashes and rouge their cheeks (they never go out without their makeup), and feed them bananas, grasses and sugar cane. (They eat one quarter of their weight every day.) And for ceremonies, they're bedecked in gilded trappings. (How they get the elephants to cooperate is a mystery, and the animals must be handled gently, as they're considered avatars of future Buddhas.)

In the past, Thai monarchs desiring to bankrupt a rival would send them the gift of a white elephant or two. Beware of receiving your own "white elephant" — some unexpected or excessive concession that may, in the long (or short) run, carry disproportionate costs to your company.

Another major problem besetting companies doing business in Thailand is endemic copyright and patent infringement, not only on products but also on their packaging and logos. The government has increased its pressure on the "knock-off" trade and things are improving. Still, as Thai industry is increasingly technological (it's now a major exporter of PC motherboards), it's wise to be cautious about sharing patented technologies without specific guarantees of, and explicit plans for, protection against copyright infringement.

Contracts, Thai Style

In developing countries, changes can be rapid or take unexpected turns. Foreigners shouldn't be surprised if their deal undergoes odd and rapid erosions. It's best to anticipate changes by trying to build into your contract a high degree of flexibility in any areas that won't actively harm your business. A contract should be as precise as possible about finances, deadlines and standards and, at the same time, as loose as possible about nonessentials. It should also be fairly brief in duration and include a limited-time escape clause.

Thais generally respect contracts. However, they also view agreements as attachments to the people who signed them. To Thais, a handshake carries more weight than a written document. To ensure success, arrange to have a team member on-site for the duration of your project.

13

Business Outside the Law

Underground Economy

In Thailand, the underground economy is not a product of outsiders or urban slums. It penetrates every level of society. It's noteworthy, however, that the social gap is widening. The top 20 percent of the population earns 87 percent of the national income (up from less than 50 percent twenty years ago.)

Extralegal activities are mainstays of the economy. Thailand has a vast panoply of taxes, direct and indirect, most of them very high by international standards. Tax fraud is ubiquitous, as are copyright and patent violations (see previous chapter).

Tourism, Thailand's single largest source of foreign currency, is fertile ground for petty scams. Direct crimes against tourists are taken seriously. However, the trade in counterfeit gems, phony antiques and fraudulent valuables (imitation Rolex and Cartier watches, Vuitton luggage, etc.) is so brisk that fakes are even graded by quality.

Prostitution, though illegal, is a major national industry. The police have been accused of complicity with crime rings that smuggle in impoverished Burmese women and girls for this purpose. While the traditional age of consent is 15, many children (of both sexes) are sold into the trade at the age of ten or younger; their number is estimated to be at least 100,000. While foreigners are often blamed for promoting the under-age trade, it's also patronized by locals, many of whom believe that prepubescent children aren't capable of carrying AIDS. Ironically, sex tourists from the Middle East believe that deflowering a prepubescent will actually *cure* AIDS. (See "What Passes For a Nightclub" in Chapter 20.)

Drugs (from Golden Triangle heroin and morphine to "Thai stick" marijuana) are important cash crops. The heroin market is in decline, but methamphetamine factories are proliferating. Under pressure from the West, the government periodically cracks down on the drug trade — mainly by persecuting opium-growing hill tribes and prosecuting Western tourists caught with small amounts of "dope." Recently, however, after many delays, the government extradited "Thai Tony," a former top government official accused of large-scale drug-dealing in northern California.

Although criminal gangs exist, organized crime (on the scale of Japan's Yakuza) isn't a great problem. (Incidentally, tattoos don't indicate gang membership. Many respectable Thais wear virtual art galleries on their bodies.)

Graft and Corruption

The extortion of bribes by government officials (both high and low) is so institutionalized (and resented) that it's nicknamed *kin muang* ("eating the people"). As the more talented civil servants depart for higher-paid positions in private industry, the remaining petty officials are those most likely to extract "tea money" (see Chapter 5) for petty favors. Higher officials grant larger favors in exchange for greater sums. The police have been implicated in several murders of newspaper reporters and foreign diplomats who'd been rash enough to investigate police corruption. Even the Army is suspected of corruption — thought to be colluding with the Khmer Rouge in the illegal trade of gems and endangered-species timber.

In 1995, one Thai politician was charged with buying over 200,000 votes for himself at a cost of 56 million *baht* (approximately US$2.24 million). Such funds are often "black" monies — profits from illegal gambling operations, the drug trade and extorted "rents" from local shopkeepers. According to the *Far Eastern Economic Review,* canvassers in rural areas went door-to-door handing out over US$1 billion worth of *baht* to the citizenry during Thailand's November 1996 national election. Some voters claim to have been intimated into making the "right" choice by soldiers and off-duty policemen. The problem has led to the creation of Pollwatch, a national volunteer group of about 45,000 "watchdogs" whose budget (US$3.1 million) comes from government coffers.

With Thailand's tolerant ethics and laissez-faire government, corruption is likely to remain engraved in Thai life, no matter how many military coups claim to end it. (As previously mentioned, eighteen such "anti-corruption" coups have occurred since 1932.) Still, with a thriving economy that's increasingly dependent on international goodwill, Thailand's high-end business class is becoming more and more fed up with such illicit tactics, and more and more vocal about the need for change.

NARINCHAI
CHIDCHOB

14 Names & Greetings

Thai names are usually multisyllabic, and (as in Chinese) each syllable has a meaning or symbolism. They follow Western order, with the given name first. Family names were introduced by Royal Decree in 1913 by King Vajiravudh, who was much taken with Western ways and considered Thailand's lack of genealogy uncivilized. But Thais were so bewildered by the law that the king had to personally coin patronymics for hundreds of families, who couldn't imagine what they were supposed to call themselves. Even today, these family names are rarely used.

Nicknames are common, often given at birth and used throughout one's life. Visitors may be given one, too, especially if their names are hard for Thais to pronounce. The formal, all-purpose, gender-free honorific is *Khun* (for Ms., Mr., etc.). Expect to be called *Khun Barbara* or *Khun Ed*, with all respect, in return. (Thai monks have a different, hierarchic set of titles, but you're unlikely to need to know them.

Family designations include: *pee* (elder brother or sister); *nong* (younger brother or sister); *phoo* (paternal grandfather) and *yaai* (maternal grandmother). However, these are sometimes used for people who aren't related. *Nong,* for instance, may be used to address a young waiter in a restaurant.

Greetings

The Thai greeting is the *wai* (similar to India's *namaste*), a bow of the head with fingers pressed together prayerfully in front of the face. More than a greeting, it's also a symbol of respect; you'll see Thais making this gesture when they pass shrines. The higher the hands are placed, the more respect is signified (but the forehead's the limit). The *wai* is given to a peer or a superior, but never to an inferior. (If you return your hotel maid's *wai*, she'll think you're an ignorant *farang*.) The correct response to a *wai* from someone of lower status is a smile and a nod.

In general, Westerners shouldn't use the *wai* in business relationships. Thais will expect you to shake hands (use right hand only), and you may certainly initiate the handshake.

 Communication Styles

What's In A Smile?

Since the Thai are exquisitely tactful, even in the face of serious *faux pas* by *farang* guests, they will not tell you when you've erred. You'll have to learn on your own by watching what others do and how they react nonverbally to your behavior.

Thailand is called "The Land of Smiles," but a smile can mean many things. Often, it indicates genuine friendliness, as Thais are indeed warm and hospitable. During negotiations or when tensions are otherwise building, they'll smile or joke to relieve tension and restore group harmony. A noncommittal smile may also conceal negative thoughts, indicate passive resistance to pressure for a decision, or forestall saying "no" directly.

As in most of Asia, a nervous giggle indicates embarrassment. It may often be the only overt signal you'll receive that you're causing somebody emotional distress. A sudden brief laugh for no apparent reason is a frequent reaction to *farang* rudeness. Chinese-Thais who maintain close Chinese ties may even guffaw unpleasantly when someone suffers an awkward moment. This actually conceals (but simultaneously disowns) empathetic pangs at another's "loss of face" or decorum; it also serves to chase off any evil spirits attracted by human embarrassment. Thais may also smile or laugh in sad or tragic situations, as a way of covering up their sorrow.

Be aware that though Thais are highly tolerant of the ways of others, they may silently rise and walk out if offended. If that happens, you'll know that you have problems.

16   Customs

Gifts

Gift-giving is a normal procedure when you're invited to someone's home, and it's also very much a part of business life. Thais love beauty — to the point that the laundries giftwrap clothing they've cleaned — so have your gifts wrapped exquisitely, in vibrant colors.

At your exploratory visit with a company, bring inexpensive office gifts (such as pens or datebooks with your logo). Once your relationship is established, bring a more valuable gift for the senior officer. You may also choose gifts (such as sweets) that can be shared throughout the office.

Gifts should be of good quality, but not so expensive as to leave the recipient with a burdensome obligation. (Government officials receiving "tea money" or its equivalent in gifts won't be bothered by such subtleties, however.) Roses and tulips are fine, but carnations and marigolds are for funerals and lotus flowers for temple offerings. Other choices include European chocolates, quality toiletries, cigarettes, a book augmented with photographs about your native city, or a bottle of wine from your home country. (Also, Johnny Walker Black Label scotch is a favorite.) Always give gifts in person; they don't count as much when you send them.

Refusing a gift is an extreme insult. Western rules against being "corrupted" by gifts from business contacts are considered rude and uncouth. Thai life is still communitarian, with the workplace an extension of village life; the separation of business from pleasure and of business relationships from friendships strikes Thais as unnatural. If you're concerned about the obligation, reciprocate with a gift of equal value at the next opportunity, or treat the giver to dinner. When receiving a gift, don't open it in the giver's presence unless you are emphatically urged to do so. Peel away the gift-wrap gently, and with respect.

And when shopping, remember that there are very strict laws governing the export of Buddha images. Those that have been blessed by senior monks are considered sacred.

Amulets and Tattoos

Many Thai wear small, good luck Buddhist amulets that have been blessed by monks. Never touch (or ask to touch) someone's amulet. Tattoos are thought to have similar powers (and in no way indicate, as in some other cultures, that the bearer is a thug). Among the Karen, a hill tribe with especially burdensome ancestor-worship rituals, tribe members who convert to Buddhism believe that tattoos will free them from their ancestor spirits.

For a few *baht*, non-Thais can garner a bit of good luck for themselves by purchasing a tiny, live sparrow (or two). They're sold in the countryside in little mesh purses for the express purpose of being set free. Open the latch and watch them fly off into the tree-covered hills.

Songkran

Thailand has numerous festivals through the year, most either religious or celebrating seasonal agricultural milestones. Each region has additional festivals of its own. Among the prettiest festivals nationwide are *Maha Puja* in February and *Visaka Puj* in May. Both are celebrated with the release of caged birds, incense-burning, and candle-lit processions around Buddhist temples. *Songkran*, the three-day Thai New Year (usually mid-April), was originally a time for cleaning household Buddha images, presenting small gifts, and for blessing one's family and friends by sprinkling a little white powder and then a little perfumed water on them (an ancient purification ritual with roots in Hinduism). Today, at the very height of the hottest, driest season, the celebration becomes a mass water fight, which leaves everybody deliciously soaked. Westerners are a prime target for buckets of cold water (and high-powered water pistols), so be prepared.

At *Songkran* 1995, however, the environs of Bangkok became the site of the now-legendary "mother of all traffic jams." On the eve of the holiday, bumper-to-bumper traffic bound for the airport and the countryside reached total gridlock for a full forty-eight hours. Whole families spent the weekend in their cars, while others abandoned their vehicles on the road and walked or hitchhiked home. One moral of the story is: if you're in Bangkok at *Songkran*, don't plan on traveling. Just get out and have fun.

Loy Krathong

Historically, canals and rivers played a major role in daily life, providing irrigation, transportation, fish for the table, etc. This holiday, an animistic festival to propitiate water spirits (and prevent floods), is a time for giving thanks to, and asking forgiveness of, Mae Kongkha, the Mother of Waters. On a full moon night in October or November, when the rivers are at their height, incense, lit candles, coins and flowers are set afloat in banana-leaf boats (*krathong*), creating magical scenes throughout the country.

Weddings

Upon registering with a local district office, a couple becomes legally married. More romantic is the blessing that follows. The bride and groom, dressed in traditional costume, kneel side by side. A *mongkol* (a thick white cotton thread) is wrapped around their heads, symbolizing their union, then guests sprinkle scented water on the couple's hands. (Astrologers are consulted to ascertain the most auspicious dates and times for these events.) An evening reception usually follows.

17 Dress & Appearance

Business

Thais place high value on personal hygiene and cleanliness, and they regard clothing as a measure of status. Wearing conservative business attire, despite the tropical heat, indicates your serious intent. Men should wear dark suits (jackets can usually be removed during meetings), although Thai counterparts may wear shirtsleeves with a tie. Black is a mourning color, but for formal occasions, women may choose a black dress if it's accented with color. Knees and shoulders should be covered (except at the beach), no matter how hot it is. Fortunately, stockings and pantyhose aren't expected.

Although most business sites are air conditioned, the heat, smog and slow transit en route may necessitate several complete changes of clothing per day. Pay special attention to fresh, hole-free socks, as you'll be expected to remove your shoes in homes and some restaurants. (Loafer-style shoes come in handy.) Hotel laundries are usually quick and careful. Ready-made clothing in Western sizes is available; and if you're staying for at least a week, you can have excellent clothing custom-made at bargain prices.

During the winter, or if you're traveling in the north, bring a sweater for cool evenings, and pack lightweight rainwear for monsoon season.

Temple Protocol

"Dress Impolite Can't Enter This Temple" reads a sign, obviously directed at Westerners, in front of Chiang Mai's 14th century Wat Doi Suthep. Shorts and tank tops are inappropriate. Shoes are removed at the doorway. Religious images are often decorated with strings of jasmine flowers. Never touch them, and inquire before taking photographs. One of Thailand's most famous religious icons is the Emerald Buddha. The King personally changes its robes every four months to correspond with the seasons.

Casual & Ethnic Attire

Thai men often wear *maw hawn*, loose white cotton overshirts and blousy white pants. When relaxing or dressing up, women may don long, beautifully printed sarongs or caftans made of lightweight cotton or silk.

Northern hill tribes have their own distinctive fabrics (often embroidered or appliquéd), jewelry, and headgear, ranging from large, square African-looking turbans of the Lisu women to the tall, silver-filigreed headdresses (encrusted with old Indian rupee coins) of the Akha, a small tribe poor in goods but rich in jewel-craft. In some localities, the women change their everyday clothing after marriage, adopting a different head-dress, different jewelry or a different cut of skirt.

Reading the Thai

Nine Do's and Taboos

1. Don't Touch Heads

Thai etiquette concerning heads and feet is as emotionally loaded as social rules about private bodily functions are in the West. The head is considered the holiest part of the human body, because its the seat of *khwan*, one's spirit. (Barbers give a *wai* before cutting someone's hair.) Never touch anyone's head. Firmly combat any impulse to pat a child's pate. (The Thais believe it will unleash mischievous spirits that will wreak havoc.) When passing in front of another person, especially an older one, lower your upper body slightly, as a symbolic means of equalizing the height of your heads.

2. Don't Show Feet

Conversely, feet are considered utterly base. Be careful not to point your toe, heel, or sole at anyone, not even at an animal, or to move objects with your foot. (A few years ago in an American nightclub, a Thai immigrant murdered a Laotian because the Laotian had stretched his foot toward the Thai's girlfriend, who was dancing on stage.) Sit with your legs tucked behind you or to the side. Don't stretch out when seated in an armchair, and avoid crossing your legs, lest you reveal your unworthy sole. Putting your feet up on a chair or table is so taboo that it can instantly end a budding relationship.

3.   Speak Quietly, Walk Softly, Gesture Gently

As a rule, English-speaking people (particularly males) pitch their voices more loudly and deeply than Southeast Asians, and they may try to overcome language barriers by turning up the volume. Try to quiet down and slow down, giving your Thai listeners the time to hear and assimilate your message.

Americans tend to gesture expansively. In contrast, when Thais "speak with their hands," they speak very softly. When in Thailand, try to make your posture and motions compact and dignified, rather than loose or (regardless of your gender) aggressively masculine. Don't clomp when you walk. Never stand talking to someone with your hands in your pockets (a rudeness that rises to the level of vulgarity if you also fiddle with your loose pocket change). Thais will overlook a hapless *farang's* heavy tread or graceless posture, but if Thailand is likely to play a large part in your future, studying a martial art such as tai ch'i may help you learn to appear less uncouth.

Pointing with one finger is considered aggressive, and therefore impolite. Instead, gesture with your chin and head. To beckon, stretch out your arm, palm down, and make a scooping motion with your fingers. Finger-snapping, excessive hand-flapping, and sibilant hissing are all considered coarse.

4.   Listen and Wait

Listen carefully and wait for others to finish. Don't interrupt anybody, including others on your own team. In serious discussions, Thais sometimes take a moment to think before speaking, and you may do so, too. That brief silence may allow you to choose polite words to phrase some potentially-unflattering concern. Even if you're eager to express a sudden great idea, rein in your impatience. Remember to keep a "cool heart."

5. Physical Space, Social Space

Thais have had sufficient experience with *farang* tourists and businesspeople to observe the relatively large "personal space" that Westerners and Japanese keep around them. If your relationships mellow into friendships, physical distance is likely to shrink to slightly less than you're accustomed to, although not to a disquieting proximity. In crowds (e.g., on buses), Asians generally won't sit half-off the bench (like Westerners) to avoid body contact with a seatmate. The other person simply doesn't exist for the time being.

6. Physical Contact: Different Rules Apply

Although any public display of romantic affection is considered scandalous, Thais are often physically affectionate with friends of the same sex. It's not uncommon to see a pair of men or boys, women or girls holding hands as they walk. This doesn't imply homosexuality (although Thailand is very tolerant about sexual orientation). It is, in fact, the *absence* of homophobia that allows this same-sex physical contact. If your relationships with Thai colleagues deepen into friendships, they may touch you more often than would a same-sex colleague at home. If this makes you uncomfortable, you can simply fail to respond, and Thais will understand that you're just a typically cold, stiff *farang*. If, however, you behave as if you're repulsing an offensive sexual approach, they'll be deeply insulted.

Conversely, the West's playful-aggressive "friendly" touches are unacceptable. Don't slap or pat any Thai on the shoulders or back (unless he does it to you first), or hug him to show appreciation. Never place your arm over the back of a chair that somebody's sitting in. And never throw or even toss something to another person (except when playing ball); hand the item over, preferably with your right hand (or with both hands, to show respect).

7.   Respect the Monarchy

Stringent laws guard against showing disrespect to the royal family, which is regarded with adoration. (In early 1996, millions watched the cremation of the king's mother and observed a 100-day mourning period by wearing black.) You'll receive dirty looks or even a scolding from onlookers if you step on a dropped coin, thereby placing your foot on the engraved image of the king's face. Even if you hear Thais quietly voice some concerns about the current line of succession, keep any critical thoughts to yourself.

8.   Honor Religious Protocol

Thais gain karmic merit by giving food and donations to members of religious orders. However, a woman must not touch a monk, or even hand him anything directly. Instead, lay the object before him, or have the nearest male hand it to him. It's considered disrespectful to stand near a seated monk.

9.   You're Nobody's Great White Rajah

Many Caucasians have a tendency (conscious or not) to assume a certain superiority over darker-skinned "natives," even in cultures that are older, wiser, and richer in the arts and religion than their own. Often, this patronizing approach is quite subtle. It can only serve to undermine your relationships.

19 Entertaining

Passionate Palates

Thailand is a nation of fervent gourmets, and those "cool hearts" have passionate palates.

A typical Thai dish is a whole carnival of flavors. While the Chinese believe in *balancing* "the five tastes" (sweet, sour, bitter, salty, and spicy), Thai cooks *combine* all five — and then some. Ginger, garlic, hot pepper, basil, coriander leaf, mint, lemongrass and coconut are the basic seasonings. (Coconuts are harvested from trees by trained monkeys — "no strikes, no holidays, no unions," as one Thai put it — at the rate of 500 a day). Fish sauce (*nam pla*) is a staple flavoring and a table condiment for rice. Made from fermented dried anchovies or squid, it's slightly pungent-smelling in the bottle but mellows into a subtly aromatic saltiness when combined with other ingredients.

Ingredients are usually chopped, ground, or shredded. This practice originated in China to conserve scarce fuel (a few twigs burning hot and fast stir-fry a whole meal). Many dishes are spicy, very spicy, or incendiary, with the heat a coloratura high note in the polyphonic flavor-chorus. If you dislike piquant foods, specify *mai ped* ("not spicy"). If you like it, you may find the food "blanded down" at Western-style hotels. Nonetheless, be careful about consumption of the tiny, searing *phrik leung* ("rat droppings") chilies. Rice, yoghurt or something sweet (even a spoonful of sugar) will decrease the peppers' sting.

Meals may begin with intriguing appetizers, such as *ma haw* (spicy minced meat on pineapple slices). Thai soups are remarkable for their complexity, often managing to be sour, spicy, and yet comforting all at once. Salads often include some seafood, meat or poultry, and live up to their Thai name, *yum*. *Kai yang* is barbecued chicken stuffed with grated coconut. *Gaeng ped* is a curry of beef or chicken cooked with coconut milk, chiles and eggplant. *Hom-mok* is fish steamed in coconut juice, curry and coriander. You'll also be offered "clay pots" (thin stews similar to their Chinese cousins), as well as noodle dishes such as the celebratory *mee krob* (crisp-puffed rice noodles with sweet and sour shrimp and elaborate garnishes). Thais tend to eschew both lamb and mutton.

Culinary thrill-seekers may be able to sample frog, snake (cobra is reputedly delicious), a rat-like rural rodent, sugared eggs containing unborn chicks, and other exotic fare. Morning glories are believed to improve one's eyesight, and water lily stems are cooked with coconut milk and fish. Food at street-stands and marketplaces is generally safe, but raw shellfish is risky (due to untreated sewer discharges). Northeastern Thailand specializes in frog legs, and Chiang Mai in minced-meat roll-ups (*larb*), which you wrap yourself from a plateful of garnishes.

Be sure to try some of Thailand's famed exotic fruits. The most unique varieties include the small hairy, ultra-sweet *rambutan* (similar to lychee) and the divine *mangosteen*, its tough maroon peel containing white sections flavored like an angelic custard. *Durian*, a massive, spiny grenade with sweet flesh, is considered a delicacy. But it has such a pungent, dirty-socks aroma that it's legally banned from hotels and airplanes. Pregnant Thai women are said to prefer sour mangoes, tamarind, and green papaya salad spiced with garlic and chilis.

Dinner in a Thai Home

Many Thai won't invite foreigners to their homes for a meal, fearing that their abodes don't meet Western standards. If you *do* have such an opportunity, bring a small gift (see Chapter 16), beautifully wrapped, and leave your shoes at the door. You may also bring small gifts for the children of the household, especially on repeat visits. Guests may (and should) offer compliments on the home but should avoid overpraising any particular object, as the hostess may feel obliged to give it to you. Don't offer to help in the kitchen, at least not until a friendship is fully developed.

You'll usually sit on the floor around a table. Men sit cross-legged, women with their legs tucked to the side and behind them. Try a little of everything, so as not to offend your host, and be prepared for very spicy food. Dessert, if it's offered, will probably be fresh fruit. Coffee is usually the instant variety.

The Restaurant Meal

Unlike in the West, some of the best meals (including lavish buffets) can be found in hotel restaurants. Food from nearly every nationality is available. Some restaurants display food samples in the window. Smaller local restaurants charge foreigners a higher price, but the difference is minor.

(In Bangkok, those with a craving for Western fast food can choose McDonald's, Mr. Donut, Pizza Hut, Kentucky Fried Chicken, as well as Swensen's, Haagen-Daz and Sizzler Steak House.)

Restaurant tabs are never split. (Thais are amused by this weird *farang* custom, which they call "American share.") And never fight over the check. The "senior" person hosts ("senior" can apply to age, wealth or professional rank); guests can reciprocate by hosting another dinner, or by contributing a bottle of good liquor. If you're the senior person, you *must* act as host and toastmaster — not only paying the bill but also drawing everyone at the table into the conversation.

The host leads the way into the restaurant. Most restaurants have tables and chairs, but in some old-fashioned northern-style restaurants, guests remove their shoes and sit on floor-cushions or low stools arrayed around a low table. Meals are served "family style," with several dishes arrayed in the center of the table. In Thai food establishments, forks and spoons will be provided; knives are rarely used. Chopsticks are for noodles and Chinese restaurants. Wait for your host to serve or to signal you to start, and don't begin eating until he or she does.

Men are served before women. If each of you serves yourself, always use the serving spoon to take food from a communal plate, never the cutlery you've eaten from. First place a heap of rice on your plate. (Thailand's long-grain "jasmine rice" has a near-floral fragrance and nutty taste. In northern regions, a shorter-grained sticky rice is preferred.) Then spoon a small amount of one or two main courses on your rice. When you're done with that, take a small amount of another dish. Piling everything on your rice at once diminishes the distinctive pleasures of each dish, and taking large portions the first time around is considered boorish. When you're finished eating, always leave a little food on your plate; a clean plate signals that you're still hungry.

Most Thais eat with a spoon in the right hand and a fork in the left hand (for pushing food into the spoon). You'll be forgiven if you eat like a foreigner, as long as you're otherwise gracious. In the north, many people eat with their fingers, rolling some sticky rice into a ball and squeezing it around mouthfuls of the main course. Avoid touching any food with your "unclean" left hand, except to hold fruits you're peeling.

The Thai social meal is a long, convivial talk-fest. Lunches can run to two hours, dinners to three, and the latter may segue (for the males, at least) into a night on the town.

Smoking & Tipping

Many Thai smoke tobacco, sometimes all through the meal as well as afterwards. It's considered offensive to ask smokers to desist on your behalf. If you smoke, offer your cigarettes around the table before lighting up. Though Thai women don't traditionally smoke or drink in public, Western women are free to indulge.

If you're the only smoker in the group, follow the usual protocols about asking before puffing, as a degree of health-consciousness is gradually making an appearance into Asia.

Because a service charge is almost invariably included, tipping isn't customary. However, you may wish to add on 10 to 15 percent when you're the host.

Sino-Thai Eating Customs

Chinese Thais run much of the business in Thailand, and there are many Chinese restaurants serving South China's artful, savory cuisine. These are good choices for those unable to handle hot pepper.

If you successfully do business with a Chinese-Thai company, you're likely to be the guest of honor at a dinner, in which case you'll be seated facing the door. At formal Chinese meals, a roast fowl (chicken or duck) may be the centerpiece, and as the honoree you'll probably be served the head, halved, with the inner portion facing you. This is not a test — but if you turn green, you'll "lose face." Take a few tastes and "save" face. The prized delicacy is the tiny bird-brain, creamy and mild-flavored.

Drinking at Meals

Drinking usually begins when the first course is served. The table monitor stationed next to your group will pour one finger (about a capful) of liquor into each diner's tumbler, and will top it off with plentiful ice and soda. Wait for your host to begin drinking before you do. If there's toasting, you won't be expected to empty your glass in one gulp. Whenever anyone's glass is half-empty, the monitor will refill it.

Mekhong is a Thai rice whisky. You can also order local brews, which are light lagers. Alcohol is efficacious at dissolving the oils of the chile pepper, but if you want something else to gulp, soft drinks and bottled water are available. (Avoid drinking tap water.) The "Thai iced tea" and "Thai iced coffee" so popular in Thai restaurants in the U.S. are, in Thailand, considered more as desserts than mid-meal beverages.

20 Socializing

Generosity is a Virtue

Thais conduct at least as much business outside of their offices as in them. A distaste for routine, a love of *sanuk*, and the emphasis on personal relations as the basis of business all work together to make some of the most important meetings the ones held around dining tables.

Always keep in mind that generosity is highly prized. Don't be embarrassed by the lavishness of Thai hospitality (if not in cost, then in care, considerateness, and the attempt to find special treats for you to experience.) When it's your turn, reciprocate in kind. Squeezing *bahts* will lose you both "face" and business.

Conversational Guidelines

- Refrain from discussing or even mentioning *The King and I*. The Broadway musical, movie and book are all banned and widely despised because of their condescending portrayal of one of Siam's most progressive monarchs.

- Don't talk about the royal family or Thai politics, and avoid excessive zeal when expressing any negative opinions.

- Thais enjoy mildly ribald jokes, but frank or frequent discussion of sex is considered highly improper.

- You may respectfully ask questions about Thai religious beliefs and practices. But avoid any criticisms about practices you disagree with or view as superstitions.

- Avoid discussing topics like literature, art and music with people who aren't well-educated.

- Thais are likely to ask foreigners highly personal questions that they consider perfectly polite — your age, how much money you make, how much you paid for your watch, and so on. If you don't want to answer, respond with a joke or a clever counter-question ("How old do I look?"). You may ask them the same sort of questions.

Sports

Jogging and golf have taken Thailand by storm. Despite Bangkok's choking air pollution, joggers are found in every park. Golf signals, and increases, high status, and it's played by the wealthiest business class. Golf club memberships can cost US$25,000, but Bangkok has a number of public driving ranges. If you know how to play, and expect to meet this class of people, bring your clubs, or inquire about the possibility of renting them from your hotel.

Tennis is also moderately popular, although Thais consider it somewhat unseemly for foreigners to work up a sweat. In fact, if you're involved in any Thai game, remember that it's supposed to be *sanuk*. Play for the sake of play, not slaughter. (You don't have to throw the game, but avoid intense competitiveness unless your playmate exhibits it.) Other participation sports you may witness are *tai ch'i* (mainly a pastime of the aged), elaborate kite "battles," and several types of ballgames (including *tackraw*, an elaborate cross between volleyball, kickball and tumbling that uses a ball made of rattan).

Familiar spectator sports include baseball, soccer and horse races. More popular yet is *Muay Thai* (Thai Boxing), a picturesque form of kickboxing that dates back to the Middle Ages. (Despite their low regard for the foot, Thais enjoy numerous sports that center on its use.)

Cockfighting, beetle-fighting and fish-fighting are officially illegal because of the excessive gambling surrounding them; nonetheless, your colleagues may find some matches for you, or you may happen upon them. (Gambling is practically *the* national sport. Thais will wager on anything from the fastest cockroach in a street-cockroach race to the winning team in the World Cup.) Bullfights between two bulls are popular in the far south.

Not quite a sport, but a well-liked pastime when hosting foreigners, is booking a boat and spending several hours exploring the riverways and *khlongs* (canals) of Bangkok or other cities.

Movies

Bangkok has recently developed its own full-fledged film industry. Only thirty years ago, most Thai films were silent, shot on 16 mm stock, and accompanied in the theater by a live narrator/musician. Nowadays, Thai movies look more like their Hollywood cousins, but the stories have "village" rather than "urban" appeal. A few basic, unsophisticated plots (comic romance across economic lines, slapstick, or chop-socky action films) are mainstays. There are no subtitles, but then, subtitles may not be necessary once you've seen a few. More popular among Bangkok residents are American movies (especially blood-splashed action epics) and martial arts films from Japan and Hong Kong, the latter subtitled in English.

Demise of the Classics

Performances by a classical Thai orchestra (*phi pat*) can still be found, but generally, homegrown pop music is what flourishes among urban Thais. (However, several hill tribes remain enthusiastic folk musicians, with young males courting their partners with homemade instruments and traditional love songs.) The most distinctive Thai performance art form, puppetry (utilizing life-size puppets) has disappeared almost entirely as a living art, existing only as a "culture show" for travelers. It's still possible (and thrilling, if your tastes are so inclined) to attend performances of *lakhon* (see Chapter 3, p. 13).

Craft & Floating Markets

Among Thailand's best-known crafts are elaborate Meo (Hmong) needlepoint (embroideries and appliques that decorate garments, purses and pillowcases) and delicate silver jewelry. With luck, you may also find some highly striking jewelry made by the most remote of the hill tribes for their own adornment. (The metals aren't pure, but the artistry is great.) Finely-made baskets, fans and lacquered home accessories are also popular purchases. By all means, plan to visit a large marketplace, such as the Weekend Market in Bangkok, at least once. Not only will you be able to buy such crafts to take home, but the homegrown songs and chants that many stallholders sing to attract customers are quintessentially Thai. Bangkok's famous Floating Market and the newer Kha Floating Market feature local fruit, vegetables and souvenirs.

What Passes For a Nightclub

Most Thai bars, karaoke bars and nightclubs are essentially sex establishments, though visitors need not actively participate. Many an informal business dinner in Bangkok turns into a round of bar-hopping in the Patpong district, which consists of three streets. Patpong 1 features glittery nightclubs and heavy hustling. Patpong 2 is famous for massage parlors and caters mainly to English-speaking tourists. Patpong 3 hosts transvestite extravaganzas and tends to attract a Japanese clientele. Loud music, scantily-clad or nude B-girls and dancers are featured. (Many are provincial girls hoping to earn enough money after a few years to return home and set up a dress shop or hair salon.) Have a drink on the ground floor, or venture upstairs for highly provocative (or scandalous, depending on your perspective) floor shows, and be prepared to pay a highly provocative fee. This form of nightlife is directed toward men, but women tourists are free to visit.

There are three other factors about Thailand's sex industry that foreigners should be aware of.

- First, the pretty girl who calls to you on the street may actually be an artful boy.

- Second, in Thailand's Buddhist culture, a prostitute isn't considered spiritually disgraced; hence, sex workers maintain a certain inner dignity, and those who are sufficiently young, pretty and healthy-looking to work in the bars will turn down potential clients they dislike. Often, they'll make arrangements that last the length of a favored client's stay.

- Finally, you probably have a 30 percent chance of contracting a fatal disease from unprotected sex. The strain of AIDS prevalent in Thailand is heterosexually transmitted in both directions. It's so virulent that it has already begun contributing to a nationwide labor shortage that's expected to become acute in the next decade. The Thai government is currently waging an AIDS education campaign via print and TV. (Condoms have been nicknamed *mechais,* after Mechais Viravaidhya, the dynamic women who runs the campaign.)

Other Nightlife

Regular, sex-free bars where people socialized were, until recently, the exception rather than the rule. Today, alternatives include the music bars in large hotels and Bangkok's highly popular jazz clubs. Several establishments offer traditional Thai music and dancing. A half-dozen Bangkok "cyber-cafes" offer ice cream, cake or coffee along with Internet access. And two dozen of Bangkok's temples, monuments and palaces have recently been equipped with spotlights for nighttime viewing.

Chiang Mai's Night Bazaar offers everything from three-metal bronzeware and Burmese tapestries to Chanel T-shirts, and it's an interesting place for people watching. You may see a five-year-old hill tribe girl, dressed in an elaborately pleated and embroidered dress, standing in front of a TV screen — mesmerized by old clips of Elvis Presley crooning out "Heartbreak Hotel."

21 Basic Thai Phrases

English	Thai
Yes No	*Chai* *Mai*
Hello/Good-bye	*Sawasdee krap (man)* *Sawasdee ka (woman)*
Where is…?	*Yu nai … ?*
I wish to go to …?	*Yak ja pai…*
Thank you	*Kawkhun krap (man)* *Kawkhun ka (woman)*
Please	*Dai prod*
Excuse me I don't understand	*Khor tawt* *Pom mai kao jai*
You're welcome	*Yindee*
Do you speak English?	*Khun poot pasa angrit dai mai krap? (man)* *Khun poot pasa angrit dai mai ka? (woman)*
How much does this cost?	*Ni raka towrai?*

Addresses are like those in the West, but with postal codes and street numbers (of large buildings and major government ministries) often omitted. A typical address:

Khun Linchong Limpigomolchai
Bank of Thailand
273 Samsen Road
Bangkok

Mail can be sent from any large hotel, and *poste restante* (general delivery) can be used to receive mail. (You'll need to show your passport when picking it up.) When sending packages, do so from large post offices, not the ones in small villages, and send them by registered mail.

All international couriers (including Federal Express, United Parcel Service and DHL) have branch offices in Bangkok.

23 Useful Numbers

Red public telephones can be found on the street and in some shops and hotels. Some use two one-*baht* coins, others require tokens.

- Thailand country code ....[66]
- International access code from Thailand ...001
- International operator 235-0030
- Bangkok city code ....(02)
- Chiang Mai city code ....(053)
- Bangkok Police .... 191 or 123
  Tourist Police .... 195 (for English dial 1699)
- Ambulance 252-2171-5
- Local information 13
- Long distance information.......... 101 or 183
- Tourist information centers:
  Bangkok 280-1305, 282-8129
  Korat/Nakhon Ratchasima ..... (044) 213-666
  .... (044) 213-030
  Chiang Mai ....(053) 248-604, 248-607
  Khon Kaen .... (043) 244-498
- Bangkok International Airport (Don Muang)
  .... 535-1111, 535-1253 (domestic)
- Chiang Mai Airport .....(053) 211-541, 210-043
- Hualampong Railway Station 233-0341
- Thai Foreign Trade Dept. 223-1413
- Thai Chamber of Commerce 221-3351

Books & Internet Addresses

Travelers' Tales: Thailand, edited by O'Reilly & Habegger. Travelers' Tales, Inc., San Francisco, California, 1993. Sharp, funny insights about Thai life by major Western and Thai writers.

Doing Business With the Thais, by Paul Lepper. Patton Pacific Press, Sebastopol, California, 1992. A close look at Thai business culture.

Lords of the Rim: The Invisible Empire of the Overseas Chinese, by Sterling Seagrave. Putnam, New York, 1995.

Thailand, Buddhist Kingdom as a Modern Nation-State, by Charles S. Keyes. Westview Press, Boulder, Colorado, 1987). Definitive, well-written.

A Common Core: Thais and Americans, by John Paul Fieg. Intercultural Press, New York, 1989. Explores the differences and similarities between Western and Thai cultures.

Video Night in Kathmandu, by Pico Iyer. Random House/Vintage, New York, 1988. A humorous, often poignant look at culture clash in Thailand and other Asian countries. An instant classic.

The Legendary American: The Remarkable Career and Disappearance of Jim Thompson, by William Warren. Houghton Miflin, Boston, Massachusetts, 1970. Adventures of a highly successful American entrepreneur in Thailand.

[CD-ROM] **Four Paws of Crab, A Narrative Cookbook**, by Nora Bateson and Bancha Leelaguagoon. Live Oak Multimedia, Emeryville, California, 1994. Windows 3.1. More than a CD-ROM cookbook, this remarkable work is a visceral portrait of Bangkok in image and sound.

Internet Addresses

Discussion group
USENET: soc.culture.thai

Website run by Infoasia, a commercial firm helping Western firms start businesses in Asia
http://none.coolware.com/infoasia/

Bangkok-based homepage for Thailand, linked to other Thai websites.
http://www.nectec.or.th/

Passport to the World Series

Your Pocket Guide to Business, Culture & Etiquette

Other Passport to the World Books

- Passport ARGENTINA • Passport BRAZIL
- Passport CHINA • Passport FRANCE
- Passport GERMANY • Passport HONG KONG
Passport INDONESIA• Passport ISRAEL
- Passport ITALY • Passport JAPAN • Passport KOREA
- Passport MALAYSIA • Passport MEXICO
- Passport PHILIPPINES • Passport RUSSIA
- Passport SINGAPORE • Passport SOUTH AFRICA
- Passport SPAIN • Passport TAIWAN
- Passport THAILAND • Passport UK
- Passport USA • Passport VIETNAM

Available from your local bookseller or order direct.

 WORLD TRADE PRESS®
Professional Books for International Trade
1505 Fifth Avenue
San Rafael, California 94901 USA
Tel: (415) 454-9934, Fax: (415) 453-7980
e–mail: WorldPress@aol.com
USA Order Line: (800) 833-8586